COLQUHOUN

〜 CALHOUN

AND THEIR ANCESTRAL HOMELANDS

Ellen R. Johnson

HERITAGE BOOKS
2010

HERITAGE BOOKS

AN IMPRINT OF HERITAGE BOOKS, INC.

Books, CDs, and more—Worldwide

For our listing of thousands of titles see our website
at
www.HeritageBooks.com

Published 2010 by
HERITAGE BOOKS, INC.
Publishing Division
100 Railroad Ave. #104
Westminster, Maryland 21157

Copyright © 1993 Ellen R. Johnson

International Standard Book Numbers
Paperbound: 978-1-55613-873-7
Clothbound: 978-0-7884-8446-9

HISTORY OF THE COLQUHOUN/CALHOUN

FAMILIES

AND THEIR ANCESTRAL HOMELAND

by

Ellen R. Johnson

A genealogist will stop at nothing. She disturbs
the dead and irritates the living, in her quest for
information. There is no known cure. However the
disease is not fatal, but gets progressively worse.
From the "Munger book" by J. B. Munger

TABLE OF CONTENTS

COLQUHOUN/CALHOUN

INTRODUCTION

The past nine years of intensive research to find my family roots has been a labor of love with information found in the following libraries:

McClain Genealogy Library, Hattiesburg, MS
Genealogy Section of Hattiesburg Public
    Library
Genealogy Sections of Gulfport, Biloxi and
    Jackson, all in MS
Genealogy Section in New Orleans, LA
Mississippi Archives and History Library
Family History Center Libraries of Latter
    Day Saints in Gulfport Hattiesburg
    and in Salt Lake City, Utah
Library of Congress, Washington, D. C.

I would be remiss to overlook the many hours of assistance given to me by the volunteers   at   the   Family   History Libraries, both in MS and in Salt Lake City, Utah.

One of the very best sources for background material and lineages has come from the Genealogy Topic on "Prodigy", an on-line computer system with over one million members.   Some of the most knowledgeable people have furnished data on this COLQUHOUN/CALHOUN by answering specific queries.   In verifying the information from this source, I've found very few errors.

The most important source of information came from my family Bible given to my

father, ROBERT COLQUHOUN RANDEL, by his
mother. This originally was a gift to his
grandmother on Christmas, 1870 from her
son, Walter. Until her death the family
lineage to 1190 AD was written in her own
handwriting. Others have brought it up to
date even with my recording of RCR's death
in 1963.

Family lore was recorded verbally and in
written legacy by my father, ROBERT
COLQUHOUN RANDEL, telling of his eighty-
eight years of life. In his memory I've
written these words. He was extremely
proud to say he was a Colquhoun.

His thirty-two years of public service as
an elected county official, and service
to his church as Treasurer for over twenty
years has made a short man of 4'7" TALL.

COLQUHOUN/CALHOUN

HISTORY TO 1190 A. D.

CLAN COLQUHOUN has been an integral force
in the history of the British Isles for
many years. This community of people
were pugilistic warriors due to the
influence of their savage beginnings and
fierce neighbors. They are a hardy race
brought about by the brusque icy climate
and severe environment of the country.
Many showed great fortitude and loyalty to
their own with fearless courage. No matter
the spelling of COLQUHOUN, CALHOUN,
COLHOUN, and others, their descendants
have exhibited great courage over the past
centuries. Pride of the Clan has been and
is today their ancestral trait.

CLAN COLQUHOUN history tells us that its
origin is Pictish. Some scholars have
considered these painted skin people to be
Scythian. They were originally an Iranian-
speaking group of nomads who dominated the
various tribes populating the steppes
north of the Black Sea during the 7th
through the 4th century BC and were
blended with other peoples to create a
nation.. The writings of Herodotus and
ancient records suggest that these
wanderers originated in Central Asia or
Siberia. Moving into Caucasia in the near
East they were powerful forces until the
Medes drove them out late in the 7th
century BC.

Their tribal society was organized around
a mighty chief. Burial gravesites were
in underground chambers where the King and

1

his wife were interred. Scythian chiefs
wore and carried large amounts of gold
jewelry and weapons upon their persons
since, as travelers, the articles could
be placed in the tomb with them after
death. They kept control of the steppes
until the end of the 4th century BC when
the Sumarians pushed them back to the
Crimea. Traces of their animal-style art
were found in the barbaric art of Europe
during the early Middle Ages.

John Duran stated, "It is well established
that civilized culture existed in the
Orkney Isles (North of Scotland) at least
as early as 3200 BC. Though some
historians of either ancient times or
later would have us believe that the
Britons and their close relatives were
savages during the time just before the
Caesars of Rome ruled, this is NOT the
case. In fact as further study is done,
the Britons and the Romans are shown to be
cousins both of the descent of the Kings
of Troy. Also, the Roman Coliseum itself,
was indeed modeled after the site of that
very early British wonder- Stonehenge."

The earliest connections to the CLAN
COLQUHOUN, as shown on the chart entitled
"Origin and Variations of the Name
COLQUHOUN", were KING MILESIUS. The
Scythian line of descent to Oden 1st King
of Scandinavia (based on the LDS church
records, and appended by John Duran) shows
MILESIUS married to a daughter of
Pharoah, named Scota circa 1310 BC. His
son, Prince Heber was placed on the Throne

of Ireland, to become the first Milesian
Monarch of Ireland.

It was from King Heber that a descendant
was born in 1500 BC. He was CEALLACHAN,
pronounced as Callaghan or Kailcahan, who
became King of Munster, Ireland, thus
starting our name which has undergone many
changes in the ensuing centuries to
COLQUHOUN OR COLHOUN OR CALHOUN. His
descendents spread to many other areas of
Ireland, with all of the names being
similar to our COLQUHOUN.

The next was KING HELGE who was probably
of Scandanavian origin. These Clan Chiefs
migrated from Ireland to Scotland in 70 A.
D. No matter the method of continuation
of the narrative, current scholars have
deciphered ancient writings to provide
records of antiquity.

CALGACUS was the leader of the Caledonians
at the Battle of Mons Graupius (commonly
spelled Grampius) in A. D. 85. Tacitus
described him as "the most distinguished
for birth and valour among the
chieftains". The name is derived from
"Calg" meaning a sword. Some have given
his name to mean "swordsman". The name is
often misspelled Galgacus.

Some scholars insist that CALGACUS, who
lived circa 60-80 BC, was a COLQUHOUN who
bravely defended his country against
Agricola at the famous battle of the
Graupius. The name in Greek is rendered
as CALGACUS or Calgagius.

3

COLQUHOUN/CALHOUN

John Duran stated, "It appears that this CALGACUS was one and the same as the King of Britain, who was also known as Caradoc or Caradog or Caractacus. A king known by one name would be known by another elsewhere. To decipher the name from the Roman-Greek CALGACUS, the "us" is dropped for the Welch version with the "1" and "r" forming Caradog. The family is indeed an ancient one."

MAC A CHOUNICH (Gaelic), sometimes used as MAC A CHOMBAICH (Gaelic) and as MACACHENNICK (Gaelic), was listed before UMFRIDUS de KILPATRICK DE COLQUHOUN in 1190 A. D. was recorded as Chief. They were possibly one and the same person with equivalent names for COLQUHOUN. Other Clans and CLAN COLQUHOUN were titled Caledonians by the Romans. Caledonia is the ancient Roman name for the northern part of Great Britain north of the Firth of Forth in Highland Scotland.

Another tradition concerning the beginning of CLAN COLQUHOUN is recorded as descending from CONACH, an early Irish king sometime between 875-891 AD during the rule of Gregory the Great (Geirg'ear Mor). CONACH acquired lands from Gregory in the county of Dumbarton and named them Conochon, later renamed COLQUHOUN. The name of CONOCK (of Ireland) passed through several transitions and spellings, such as Colquhoun, Colquchoun, Colchoun, Colhoon, Cohoun and Calhoun and pronounced in all cases Co-whoon.

4

COLQUHOUN/CALHOUN

The Romans under Julius Gnaeus Agricola by 84 AD had subdued all of that part of the country south of the Firth of Forth. They built the Hadrian Wall, a line of impenetrable forts between the Forth and Clyde as a barrier against the Caledonians to keep them out of the southern provinces.

Agricola, a Roman of the imperial times, distinguished not less by his great abilities as a statesman and a soldier than by the beauty of his private character, was born at Forum Julii (Now Frejus, in Provence, France) in 37 AD. Having served with distinction in Britain, Asia, and Aquitania, and gone through the round of civil offices, he was elected consul in 77 AD and in the following year proceeded as Governor to Britain, the scene of his military and civil administration during the next seven years.

He was the first Roman general who effectually subdued the island and the only one who displayed as much genius and success in training the inhabitants to the amenities of civilization as in breaking their powerful force in war.

Roman colonists under the direction of Agricola settled in the land, built towns around their military camps, and connected these with roads which were virtually non-existent in Caledonian territory. They introduced their laws and civilization, and for the first time provided a written record of Scottish life.

Agricola died in 93 AD.

With the decline and fall of the Roman empire the legions were withdrawn to the continent, and the Britons were unable to defend themselves against the inroads of the barbarians from the North. The Germans after being requested by the Brits developed the Germanic invasion and settlement of Britain.

The Anglo-Saxon Chronicles date the principal migration at 449 AD. At that time Caledonia gradually came to be settled by the Picts, the Scots, the Britons, and Angles. All were ancestors of the Gaels of Scotland and Ireland. From the amalgamation of these four races sprang the people of modern Scotland, which acquired its name from these Gaelic invaders called the Scots or Dalriads who arrived from Ireland in the 3rd or 4th Century AD.

The strongest of the earlier inhabitants were the Celtic Picts who were known as cave dwellers sometimes living in tent-covered wagons as they traveled. Skulls found through archaeological discoveries in the 19th century disclosed the remains of men who lived in the very remote past.

When the third warm period began in the Early Stone Age, men learned to hunt and discovered the use of fire. The first stone tools were made by pounding flint for hatchets and sharpening them along the edge with hard bone. This was more than 50,000 years ago.

During the Middle Stone Age of the glacial period, the climate became cold and reindeer became plentiful. During this age men wore clothing sewed with bone needles and their cave walls were decorated with primitive drawings. New technique evolved giving them weapons of bone, wood, and flint. They even made bone whistles.

The Late Stone Age began about 10,000 BC as the 4th warm period. The women learned to plant seed and to harvest crops. Wooden homes were built besides streams and pile dwellings around lakes. Their agriculture led to permanent settlements with towns and primitive commerce. Wars began among communities and nomadic tribes arose in the country east of the Danube.

From those ages Sumerians were in Babylonia and cuneiform writing came into use.

The Picks and Scots invaded Britain in 368 AD but were defeated by Theodosius who became emperor in 379 AD of the Eastern Empire and in 392 AD, the sole emperor of the East and West. He was a zealous supporter of Christianity though waging war with friend and foe alike.

The Picts then united with the Caledonians in waging war with the Romans against the British. In the 7th century the Saxons came into conflict with them. After the Scot's conversion to Celtic Christianity, their King Angus MacFergus, ruled all Scotland for a period during the early part of the 8th century, thereby shaping a semi-peaceful existence between the warring factions.

About the beginning of the 9th century, the Picts disappeared as a separate people, leaving no literature and but scanty traces of their language. By then they had mingled with the other races. In many parts of North and West Scotland known as the Highlands a Gaelic tongue was spoken. The dialect of the South and East Lowlands had a mixture of English and Scandinavian speech.

The Pictish ancestral lineage was traced through the female as one always knew who the mother was. For that reason in the year 844 A.D. the Scots of Dalriada and Picts were consolidated into one kingdom under Kenneth MacAlpin. He had a connection to the Pictish throne through his mother, and thus was able to merge the two kingdoms.

The crown descended to Malcolm I (943-54), to Edmund I of England, and Kenneth II of Scotland (971-975). Kenneth III was succeeded in 1005 by Malcolm II, whose death in 1034 ended the male line of Kenneth MacAlpin. The crown went to his nephew, Duncan, who was brutally murdered by Macbeth thereby making himself King in 1040.

Duncan's son slew Macbeth in 1057 and regained the throne as Malcolm III. His wife, Margaret, did much to refine manners and secure justice for the poor. In 1093 he invaded England and was slain near Alnurch Castle.

MacAlpin and Macbeth were buried at St. Columba's IONA.

COLQUHOUN/CALHOUN

EARLY YEARS

The British Isles have not been successfully invaded since the Norman Conquest of 1066, but their early history records a series of settlements by people from the continent of Europe. The earliest of these before the Christian era were primarily displaced aboriginal inhabitants of the islands. It is reported that the COLQUHOUNS were among these as their mythical history suggested.

The country of Scotland, divided by mountains, seas and inland lakes together with its fertile soil, made a natural setting for the development of individual family groups of people living independent and separate lives yet being a part of the whole.

No place in Scotland is more than 70 miles from a coastline. Topographically, the country can be divided into three regions. The Highlands make up the northern two-thirds, where the highest mountain, Ben Nevis (height of 4,406') is found. The Grampian Mountains lie in the southern Highlands. Central Scotland, a lowland region with isolated hills, contains Scotland's coalfields. The southern Uplands, a region of rounded hills, is noted for raising sheep. The hills and mountains are covered with shamrock and heather, known for its beautiful purple blossoms, bracken and short grass.

COLQUHOUN/CALHOUN

With the induction of UMFRIDUS DE
KILPATRICK ET COLQUHOUN as Chief of the
CLAN COLQUHOUN, a new era was born. The
pristine beauty of the land yet unspoiled
by the blood of Clansmen was picturesque
with snow-covered mountains rising above
the villages that sprang up below. New
governments were set up Clan by Clan in an
effort to live in peace with their
neighbors. That soon was ruined with
squabbling and fighting between one Clan
or the other.

Not all of the countryside was green and
beautiful. Property north of Dumfriesshire
is Lanarkshire named for Lothus, King of
the Picts, who wore a torc, a necklace in
the form of a twisted band. The terrain,
bleak and barren on the surface, contained
vast riches of lead underneath.

At first, lead mining was seasonal for
peasants who left their homes in the
Highland country in springtime, camping in
the hills until winter drove them back.
Though it wasn't easy for those with wives
and children to leave them behind, every
able-bodied woman was needed in the
homeland. A mining camp wasn't the safest
place for the miners' families.

At the time of the Union of the Crowns
these underground riches had been nearly
forgotten but the Stuart monarchy became
rich from their deposits of gold found
in the Clyde and Nith. From Roman times,
gold has been mined in Scotland's Lowther

Hills, which is sometimes called "God's Treasure House".

In 1613 Bevis Bulmer, a professional gold hunter, was able to supply Queen Elizabeth I of England with a porringer of Lowther gold. Young men with assistance from their kinfolk struggled to pan out enough gold to make a ring for their betrothed back home. Some of the artifacts of utility vessels and jewelry of gold uncovered from graves in recent years by archaeologists show their civilization was much further advanced than expected.

Disease beset the miners because of poor working conditions and the lack of a proper diet. Pack animals that carried the ore to market brought back fresh food but rarely did they return with crisp greens. Therefore, scurvy was epidemic in the camps.

Gradually the miners began working the entire year. After improving their surroundings and livelihood, they brought their families. Then the permanent settlements of Lanarkshire and its twin village, Leadhills, were established.

During the reign of Mary Queen of Scots, most of the people vulnerable to the marauders felt that life was dismal because of unrest and the wanton killings perpetrated on the citizenry. Though the situation was distressful many carried on their daily lives as though there was not a problem at all.

COLQUHOUN/CALHOUN

Peasants spent their lives working to pay homage to the King. Women feared for the lives of their husbands and sons as they went out to battle. The monarchy under the house of Caenmore, influenced from south of the border, was developing into a feudal state. After establishment of the feudal system the people were physically and economically beset by their enemies who continued to wreak havoc on the populace with no regard to the law.

To grant possession of property the Sasine act of 1617 was created to give the donee the right record, to own, and pass on inheritance to an heir. These records often give names of people, relationships, and residences, dates and sometimes references to other documents, all of which can be helpful in locating ancestors.

Before Sasine records were kept in the Notorial Protocol books. These are registered at the Scottish Record Office, P. O. Box 36, HM General Register House, Edinburgh, EHi 3YY, Scotland, UK. Some of these records are available on microfilm at Family History Centers throughout the United States.

Children were named according to the Scottish custom as follows:
First male child-father of the father.
Second male child-father of the mother.
Third male child-father's name.
First female child-mother of the mother.

COLQUHOUN/CALHOUN

Second female child-mother of the father.
Third female child-mother's name.

After that: names of uncles, brothers,
friends were in no particular order. The
format from one generation to another is
Isaac Duncan, Duncan Isaac, Isaac Duncan.
The other two possibilities: 1) The
original Duncan accomplished something
outstanding. 2) The original Duncan was a
great grandfather still alive and as
patriarch of the family his name was
honored with giving the name to the next
male heir.

All of that just to confuse the many who
are searching for their roots!

The Highlanders, who fell into a state of
poverty, instigated a new system to
protect themselves and their communities.
Strong and able men respected by their
peers were chosen as judges who settled
disputes among the people. These men were
almost autonomous even against the King's
authority. Necessary for acceptance by a
chief into his clan were the right skills
and loyalty. The Gaelic name of the Clan
may also be the name of the Clan's
progenitor and not from the Chief's name.

Frequently asked are questions dealing
with the organization of Highland Clans
and how they are determined. One of the
factors involved lies in an imaginary line
known as the highland route which runs
along the middle of the Firth of Clyde to
the southern end of Loch Lomond, then

northeast to a point some thirty miles west of Montrose and north of Dundee. It then turns north along the foothills to the mouth of the River Findhorn. From this the location of the Clan Chiefs was established as was the area of their rule.

The Clan system is unique to the Highlands of Scotland. The word Clan in Gaelic, the language which was prevalent in those days, meant "children". Although all that bore the name can not be said to have the same blood line. Anyone moving into an area would frequently place himself under the protection of the chief and take his name.

A Scot who was hunting in the hills of the north told of a escort who had been assigned to him under the name of "Gordon". He recognized him as having served as a guide on another trip using the name of MacPherson. On asking the man whether he was not the same and whether his name at the time had not then been MacPherson, the reply was, "Yes, but that was when I lived on the other side of the hill."

The Chief as spokesman for the group was responsible for the care of his people. It was a hereditary monarchy founded on custom and allowed by limited consent. Matters of importance were deferred to the other leaders of the Clans. The Chief determined answers to disputes between families, punishing or correcting injuries, supporting families in need, declaring war against or negotiating terms of peace with other clans.

The authority of the King though weak at best was powerless though still acknowledged except upon interference of disputes between the Clans. When his advice was completely disregarded, his only alternative was to beset Clan against Clan to achieve his wishes.

The warring Englishmen with their expertise in battle were able many times to cause despair in Scotland. Illiteracy of the newly settled race of people created a society where many were vulnerable to the educated Englishman. However, it was during this period of unrest that treaties known as manrent became popular. In deference to the King in the beginning loyalty was usually given to him as sovereign. Then they proceeded to do as they pleased. Scholars wrote instruments as directed by the aggrieved to be submitted to their Chief.

Each Clan, a small kingdom of its own, was commanded by its Chief with the position usually being passed to the oldest son. In a few instances brothers inherited the title, and in one case in the COLQUHOUN line it was passed through a female to her husband and back to a second son.

When going into battle, the order of the family heirdom gave the oldest son command of the right wing and the youngest the

16

rear with their father as Chief and principal commander.

Coming from the years of fighting, killing and dying, their survival had improved considerably though Clans fought Clans usually on a regular basis. Whenever the need arose to go to battle, the signal consisted of a wooden cross with one end of the horizontal piece either burnt or burning. A piece of linen or white cloth soaked with blood was suspended from the other end.

Two men each with a burning cross, were sent by the chief, each running with great speed in opposite directions. As they ran, the war cry of the clan called kin and friends to the place of the gathering named only if different than the usual place. The cross was passed from hand to hand until the territory of the Clan had been covered. General Stewart said that one of the latest instances of the fiery cross being used was in 1745 by Lord Breadalbane, when it went round Loch Tay, a distance of 32 miles in 3 hours.

A young man in preparation to become Chief had to prove his courage and valor if need be. The captain led them into the lands of some neighbor or other with whom they were presently feuding. They would then by open force bring back such cattle found, or die in the attempt. Bravery against another Clan was excused with reciprocity when their young stalwart went out to

17

fight. Once he had proven his ability, he was considered worthy to be a Chief.

When a Clan went on an excursion, they had many omens boding good or evil. If they met an armed man, they believed that good was the forecast. If they saw a deer, fox, hare, or any other four-footed beast of game, and did not succeed in killing it, that was a sign of evil. If a woman barefooted crossed the road before them, they seized her and drew blood from her forehead. The night's provisions were provided by the tenant who lived near the camp to furnish his master and the troops the necessary supplies for the night and food for his dogs.

There was a sense of family within the Clan. For hungry people food was always available from another's table. Through trials and errors in agricultural methods and new technology the Scotland of the 13th century saw improvement both for the nobility and the commoner with a more comfortable state of livelihood.

The earlier the period the harder to determine facts from legends. Unless written word can establish the difference the lore which passed from generation to generation may not in the last days resemble in any way that from the first. Such is the story of ROBERT THE BRUCE, the King of Scotland, the 7th Lord of Annandale who was half pure Celtic. He was born July 11, 1274 and died June 7, 1329. His mother, Marjorie, Countess of Carrick was in her own right of the ancient Galloway line of Fergus. (For the COLQUHOUN connection see Chart of Chiefs of CLAN COLQUHOUN. #4 SIR HUMPHREY DE COLQUHOUN).

Though the unlikelihood of this playboy born in 1298 with a silver spoon in his mouth and heir to great titles and lands being interested in fusing the people of Scotland together, that is exactly what happened. When he realized that his enemy, Sir John Comyn, the nephew of the weak deposed King John Baliol, was entering a pact with King Edward of England to establish himself on the Scottish throne with a sub-king to England, Bruce hastened to arrange his kingship in 1306 thereby slaying Comyn before the high altar of the Friars' Church at Dumfries. On March 27, 1306 Bruce was crowned at Scone. Tradition tells us he was inspired by a tiny spider. (See poem, "Try Again")

Scotland was an occupied country almost wholly under the strict and savage control of a powerful and efficient military force. Few of the nobility supported Bruce making his task almost impossible. King Edward was determined to consolidate Scotland with England. On June 24, 1314 at the battle of Bannockburn, Bruce defeated Edward II, who had succeeded Edward I in 1307. Bruce the hero and freedom fighter was great, but Bruce the King and the father of his people was greater. This care for Scotland was a duty for Bruce for the rest of his life. Bruce fought for a kingdom to gain it, hold it and strengthen it for as long as he lived.

When Britain was confronted with the possibility of merging with Scotland they were filled with anxiety at the union due to the undeniable rough and bloodstained history. One of the strongest threads throughout Scottish history is the religion knitting the people together. Who but a Scottish minister would call the King to his face, "God's sillie vassal"?

Today tourists have given the area a new reason for being. The mines closed in 1930, reopened twenty years later. The museum, a mine open to the public, and show-place cottages furnished as they were in days now gone bring in money from the frequent visitors. We're told the riches under the hills have barely been tapped. Will they bring new prosperity to the peasants?

The Patron Saint of Scotland, Andrew the Fisherman, whose feast day was the 30th of November, held a special Mass which instilled pride in the Clans. Excepts reprinted from Atlanta Celtic Festival Program Book 1987: "To me thy friends, O God, are made exceedingly powerful; their power is become very great. Yea, verily, their sound hath gone forth into all the earth, and their words unto the ends of the world. Thou shalt make them princes over the whole earth...therefore shall the people praise Thee. Truly Scotland is the

COLQUHOUN/CALHOUN

'land of the shining river, land of the
high endeavors, land of my heart forever.
Scotland the Brave.'"

TRY AGAIN
KING ROBERT BRUCE

King Bruce of Scotland flung himself down
In a lonely mood to think;
'Tis true he was monarch, and wore a
crown,
But his heart was beginning to sink.
For he had been trying to do a great deed,
To make his people glad;
He had tried and tried, but couldn't
succeed
And so he became quite sad.
He flung himself down in low despair,
As grieved as man could be;
And after a while he pondered there,
"I'll give it all up,", said he.
Now just at that moment a spider dropped,
With its silken, filmy clue;
And the King, in the midst of his
thinking, stopped
To see what the spider would do.
'Twas a long way up to the ceiling dome,
And it hung by a rope so fine;
That how it would get to its cobweb home,
King Bruce could not divine.
It soon began to cling and crawl
Straight up with strong endeavor;
But down it came with a slippery sprawl,
As near to the ground as ever.
Up, up it ran, not a second to stay,
To utter the least complaint;
Till it fell still lower, and there it
lay,
A little dizzy and faint.
Its head grew steady - again it went,
And travelled a half-yard higher;
'Twas a delicate thread it had to tread,

And a road where its feet would tire.
Again it fell and swung below,
But again it quickly mounted;
Till up and down, now fast, now slow,
Nine brave attempts were counted.
"Sure," cried the King, "that foolish
thing
Will strive no more to climb;
When it toils so hard to reach and cling,
And tumbles every time."

But up the insect went once more,
Ah me! 'tis an anxious minute;
He's only a foot from his cobweb's door,
Oh say, will he lose or win it?
Steadily, steadily, inch by inch,
Higher and higher he got;
And a bold little run at the very last
pinch
Put him into his native cot.
"Bravo, Bravo!, the King cried out,
"All honour to those who try;
The spider up there defied despair;
He conquered, and why shouldn't I?"
And Bruce of Scotland braced his mind,
And gossips tell the tale,
That he tried once more as he tried
before,
And that time did not fail.

Author Unknown

COLQUHOUN/CALHOUN

COLQUHOUN CHIEFS

1) UMFRIDUS de KILPATRICK de COLQUHOUN was born in 1190 A. D., married a COLQUHOUN, and died in 1260. He, during the reign of Alexander II, obtained a charter from MALDOUEN, THIRD EARL OF LENNOX for a grant of the lands of the Barony of COLQUHOUN in Dumbartonshire "pue servitio unius meletis" in or before 1241. (from Levenex). He therefore abandoned the name KILPATRICK and assumed that of COLQUHOUN for all posterity. UMFRIDUS could well be descended from Hundifridus, Emperor Rudulf II of Hapsburg or an abbreviated form of Gilliephadrig and later changed to Humphrey. In his day his name was pronounced Col-g-hoon.

A legend tells that UMFRIDUS DE KILPATRICK'S mother and wife were both COLQUHOUNS. From history the certainty is that the COLQUHOUN and LUSS families merged about 1400 A. D. and united two ancient families of Scotland. Since there are no written records of the LUSS family in the 1150-1190 range, tradition would probably tell us that the LUSS family descending from the COLQUHOUN family produced a strong bond between the two lines at the time of UMFRIDUS DE KILPATRICK. They had an association with the McCauslan, Luss, and Buchanan families from 1220 -1260 AD in the Dumbarton area.

2) SIR ROBERT 2ND DE COLQUHOUN was born 1220 A. D. in Dumbarton, Scotland and died

1280 in Dumbarton. At the death of his
father UMFRIDUS DE KILPATRICK AND DE
COLQUHOUN in 1260 SIR ROBERT became the
CHIEF OF CLAN COLQUHOUN. His wife's name
was unknown. Their son was SIR INGLERAMUS
3rd of COLQUHOUN. He, apparently was the
first to take his surname ROBERT DE
COLECHON, from the lands and was one of an
inspection team held at Dumbarton in 1259
(From Bain 1). Again at Dumbarton as
ROBERT DE CULCHON in 1271 he was one of
the group to discover that the daughters
of the late Finaly of Campsie were the
legal heirs of deceased Dufgall, brother
of Maldowen, Earl of Levenax. (From Red
Book of Menteith), and as ROBERT DE
COLQUHOUNE he witnessed a charter by
Malcolm, Earl of Levenax to Arthur
Galbraith around 1290. (From Levenax).

SIR ROBERT was issued a royal command to
seize the well-fortified Castle Dumbarton.
He wrote the King "Si Je Puis", meaning
"If I can". Gathering his trusted friends
and Clansmen, he organized a hunt for his
neighbors. Most of the defensive guards
from Castle Dumbarton joined the hunt
leaving the Castle unattended. Sir Robert
withdrew his men and took mastery of the
Castle without resistance. The crest of a
stag's head, indicative of the chase, was
upheld by two ratch hounds with the Motto,
"Si Je Puis". Then was born the battle
cry of the COLQUHOUN CLAN, "Cnock
Elachan".

3) INGLERAMUS 3RD DE COLQUHOUN was born
1250 A. D. in Dumbarton and died there in
1308. He ruled as Chief from 1280-1308
and lived during the reign of Alexander
III. His wife's name was unknown. In 1280
a charter of Malcolm, Fourth Earl of
Lennox, in favor of Malcolm, son and heir
of SIR JOHN de LUSS, INGLERAMUS de
COLQUHOUN was a witness. History indicates
that he probably fought against the fleet
of Norsemen from King Hakon's armed naval
force, who before the battle of Largs,
carried out a commando raid on the lands
of Lennox, dragged their boats across the
isthmus between Arrochar and Tarbet, and
burned and pillaged their way down the
loch and into the low country.

4) SIR HUMPHREY 4th de COLQUHOUN was born
1280 in Dumbarton, Scotland and died there
in 1330. He served as Chief upon the
death of his father in 1308 until his
death in 1330.His wife's name was unknown.

In 1291-92 ROBERT BRUCE and John Balliol
contended for the crown of Scotland. In
1296 Scotland submitted to England and
rebelled in 1297. Then a bloody war was
waged between them. In 1304 Scotland was
conquered by Edward I, and, even though in
1306 ROBERT BRUCE was proclaimed King, war
continued until June 24, 1314 when BRUCE
defeated the English at Bannockburn.

SIR HUMPHREY received a charter of the
Barony of Luss from KING ROBERT, the
BRUCE in 1308 for special services and on

COLQUHOUN/CALHOUN

April 26, 1308 was a witness to a charter by KING ROBERT, the BRUCE in which he is designated "UMFRIDUS de COLQUHOUN MILES". He was also a witness in the charter of Malcolm, fifth Earl of Lennox, in favor of SIR JOHN de LUSS, which was confirmed by ROBERT THE FIRST in 1316. He had charters of COLQUHOUN and Sauchie in Stirlingshire from ROBERT THE BRUCE.

From Volume I of the Accounts of the Great Chamberlains of Scotland, on July 30th 1329 quoted Mr. Tyler, "An order from KING ROBERT BRUCE created a house of COLQUHONORUM, an obscure word that appears nowhere else, and means 'Keepers of the Dogs' from the Gaelic root Gillen-an-con, and abbreviated Gille-con COLQUHOUN."

5) SIR ROBERT 5th de COLQUHOUN and 7th of LUSS, son of SIR HUMPHREY 4th was born in 1310 and died 1390. He assumed the title of Chief from 1350 to his death in 1390. Near the end of the fourteenth century he married The LADY OF LUSS, daughter and sole heiress of GODFREY (Umphredus de Luss being in the direct male line from Maldovinus de Luss) 6th LAIRD of LUSS, 1385-1415. The union in 1340 of SIR ROBERT and LADY of LUSS joined two of the prominent families of Scotland that was thereafter named COLQUHOUN of Luss. Sir Walter Scott's "Lady of the Lake" is reported to be based on six days in the life of the LADY OF LUSS. One Canto was written for each day.

27

COLQUHOUN/CALHOUN

The Fair Maid of Luss amassed the lands
from the Lord of Luss, sixth in line from
Malduin, Dean of Luss,who had been granted
the property by the 2nd Celtic Earl of
Lennox, Malduin who lived during the reign
of King William, the Lion. Thus the
ancient Clan of Luss was given to the
knight who won her hand, SIR ROBERT
COLQUHOUN of that ILK, Chief of the Clan
that had fought for KING ROBERT BRUCE.
After his battle victory SIR ROBERT was
designated "Robertus dominus de COLQUHOUN
et de LUSS" (ROBERT THE LORD OF COLQUHOUN
AND LUSS). The crest bestowed on him for
the capture of the Castle of Dumbarton was
the stag's head, indicating the chase,
supported by two ratch hounds which is the
Armorial bearing for CLAN COLQUHOUN.

After the union of the Fair Maid to SIR
ROBERT fusing LUSS to COLQUHOUN CLAN, all
kindred and followers merged to form the
one CLAN COLQUHOUN OF LUSS, whose tartan
is to be seen in various parts of the
house at Rossdhu, and also at the
COLQUHOUN Arms inn on the main road
nearby. SIR JOHN COLQUHOUN became Lord
High Chamberlain of Luss thereby obtaining
in 1368 from James III charters to create
the Barony of Luss and erecting into a
free forest the lands of Rossdhu and
Glenmachome. SIR ROBERT DE COLQUHOUN
witnessed a grant of Auchmarr from Walter
of Faslane to Walter de Buchanan in 1373
A. D. (Levenax). In 1385 the Scots invaded
England assisted by France. SIR ROBERT'S
death in 1390 occurred when his lands of
Rickle Saugh were in the hands of the

king, they not having obtained enforcement up to that time.

Their children included three sons all were born in Dumbarton:

a) SIR HUMPHREY 6th was born 1345 A. D.

b) ROBERT COLQUHOUN, the FIRST LAIRD OF THE COLQUHOUNS of CAMSTRADDEN,born in 1368 in Dumbarton, lived at Camstradden, Scotland where he secured a charter to the land of Camstradden and Achingaich. He died and was buried there in 1408. His home at Camstradden was near the Island of Inchtavanich which sheltered the area of Camstradden. Slate quarries there provided more than ample living for the COLQUHOUNS. (SEE LINEAGE CHART OF ROBERT COLQUHOUN RANDEL.)

CHIEF JOHN 6th of COLQUHOUN OF CAMSTRADDEN fought with distinction at the battle of Pinkie in 1547. There was once a castle of Camstradden but only a pile of stones remains when the Loch is very low. The COLQUHOUNS of Garscadden and Killermont were descendants from this family.

c) PATRICK, date of birth unknown, was mentioned in a charter from his brother, SIR HUMPHREY 6TH OF COLQUHOUN AND 8TH OF LUSS..

6) SIR HUMPHREY 6th OF COLQUHOUN AND 8th of LUSS was born in 1345. He ruled as Chief after the death of his father SIR

ROBERT DE COLQUHOUN 5TH OF COLQUHOUN AND
7TH OF LUSS from 1390 until his death in
1406. He was living during the reign of
King James II and was a witness to two
charters by Duncan, Earl of Lennox dated
October 28, 1395. SIR HUMPHREY 6th and
his unknown wife had five children:

a) SIR ROBERT 7TH 1406-1408,

b) SIR JOHN 8TH 1408-1439,

c) PATRICK was the ancestor of the
COLQUHOUNS of Glennis in County of
Stirling from whom the COLQUHOUNS of
Bonowfield and Piemont descend.

d) MARY lived in County Renfrew and was
married to Sir Patrick Houstan who died
1450. Mary died in 1456 and was buried
with her husband in County Renfrew.

e) CHRISTIAN lived in Glengarnock, and
married James Cunningham.

7)SIR ROBERT 7TH OF COLQUHOUN AND 9TH OF
LUSS served as Chief of CLAN COLQUHOUN for
only two years from 1406-1408.

8) SIR JOHN 8th of COLQUHOUN and 10th OF
LUSS, brother of SIR ROBERT 7TH OF
COLQUHOUN AND 9TH OF LUSS, was born in
1370 in Dumbarton, and served as Chief
from 1408 to 1439. The office of Governor
of Dumbarton Castle was awarded him in
1424 by the minor King James II for

overthrowing the powerful Lennox family. He was a patron of Parish Church of Luss where the original armorial mourning 'hatchments' of several Chiefs in the "Laird's Loft" or raised family pew in the kirk at Luss are found. He was killed at Inchmuran on Loch Lomond in 1440, ending his reign.

He married JEAN ERSKINE, daughter of LORD ROBERT ERSKINE. Children were:

a) MALCOLM COLQUHOUN, son and heir apparent of SIR JOHN 8TH OF COLQUHOUN AND 10TH OF LUSS, was born in 1395 at Dumbarton. MALCOLM was a witness in Ayr in 1429 (Ayr, pg 83). He and wife unknown had one son, John. MALCOLM was held hostage and died before his father. Therefore the Chief's title was passed to his son SIR JOHN 9TH.

b) Isabel, wed David Douglas of Mains, Scotland.

9) SIR JOHN 9TH OF COLQUHOUN and 11th of LUSS was born in 1420 and was Chief from 1459 to his death in 1478. He was Exchequer in 1460; received a charter under the great seal of several lands in 1462; received Knighthood in 1463; was Sheriff of Dumbartonshire in 1471; Great Chamberlain in 1474 and joint Ambassador to England. In 1457 his lands were brought into the free Barony of Luss, giving him local powers of life and death held by his successors until 1478. The Gallowshill

across the main road from Rossdhu marks the site of their "dule-tree".

SIR JOHN built the old castle of Rossdhu, whose ruins can be seen behind the present house, and the now roofless private chapel of St. Mary of Rossdhu.   Its beautiful mediaeval illuminated MS Book of Hours has recently been rediscovered far away among the public treasures of New Zealand.   The tomb effigy of SIR JOHN'S brother Robert COLQUHOUN, Bishop of Argyll, is now is Luss church.

SIR JOHN was killed by a cannon ball at the siege of the king's castle at Dunbar in 1478 . He married first Lady Boyd, daughter   of   Lord   Thomas   Boyd;   Their children were:

a)SIR HUMPHREY   10th of COLQUHOUN AND 12TH OF LUSS,

b)ROBERT was rector of Luss and Kippen in 1466, and consecrated Bishop of Argyll from 1473 to 1499.

c) MARGARET married William Murray, 7th Baron of Tullibardine where they lived until their death. They had seventeen sons.

JOHN 9TH became such a fervent loyalist during the Civil War that Oliver Cromwell fined him 2000 pounds.

SIR JOHN 9TH OF COLQUHOUN AND 11TH OF LUSS was married the second time in 1462 to

LADY ELIZABETH DUNBAR the second daughter of James, fifth Earl of Murray relict of Archibald 2nd son of James, 7th. Earl of Douglas. They had one son, John who was born at Dumbarton.

10) SIR HUMPHREY 10TH OF COLQUHOUN AND 12TH OF LUSS was born in 1440 and died in 1493 . He ruled as Chief from 1478 to 1493. Marriage to LADY JEAN ERSKINE, daughter of Lord Thomas Erskine produced the following children all born in Dumbarton:

a) SIR JOHN 11TH OF COLQUHOUN AND 13TH OF LUSS,

b) WALTER lived and died in Letter, Scotland,

c) PATRICK,

d) HUMPHREY lived in Letter, was married in 1528 to Elizabeth Napier and was buried in Letter.

e) ARCHIBALD died in infancy,

f) AGNES married Baron John Somerville,

g) ELIZABETH lived in Polmaise, Scotland, married James Cunningham and was buried in Polmaise.

SIR HUMPHREY COLQUHOUN 10th married second Marion Baillie.

11) SIR JOHN 11th of COLQUHOUN and 13th of LUSS was born in 1475 and served as Chief from 1493-1536. He obtained a charter of miscellaneous lands and baronies in Dumbartonshire dated Dec. 4, 1505 and received the honor of Knighthood from King James IV. He and Patrick Colhoun received a respite July 11, 1525 for assisting John, Earl of Lennox in treasonably besieging, taking and holding the Castle of Dumbarton. He married, first, LADY ELIZABETH OR MARGARET STUART, daughter of John, Lord Darnley, who became first Earl of Lennox, ancestor of the royal family of STUART by Margaret, daughter of Alexander, 2nd Lord Montgomerie. Their children were all born in Dumbarton:

a)SIR HUMPHREY 12th of COLQUHOUN,

b) JAMES,

c) WALTER lived in Craigton, Scotland and was ancestor of the COLQUHOUNS OF KILMARDINNY,

d) REV. JOHN COLQUHOUN was born in 1511, and was elected Rector of Glasgow University, Oct 25, 1553, and died in 1570.

e) MARION married SIR ROBERT BOYD. They lived in Glasgow,

f) MARJORIE (MARJORY) married SIR DUNCAN CAMPBELL. They lived in Glenurchy, Scotland,

g) CATHERINE married Duncan MacFarlane. They lived in Arrochar, Scotland.

h) AGNES was a single lady and remained in the family home at Rossdhu.

SIR JOHN 11th of COLQUHOUN AND 13TH OF LUSS married the second time to Margaret Cunningham daughter of William Cunningham of Craigends. SIR JOHN died circa August 16, 1536.

Their children were all born in Dumbartonshire:

a) THOMAS,

b) ARCHIBALD,

c) ELIZABETH,

d) GILES was born at Dumbarton, married William Chirnside and lived at Luss, Scotland,

12) SIR HUMPHREY 12th of COLQUHOUN AND 14th of LUSS was born 1495 and died at the end of January 1537. He married LADY CATHERINE GRAHAM, daughter of William Graham, first Earl of Montrose. Their children all were born in Dumbarton:

a)SIR JOHN 13TH OF COLQUHOUN AND 15TH OF LUSS,

b) JAMES of Garscube married Christian Campbell on October 28, 1558. They lived in Garscube, Scotland,

c) PATRICK married Janet Murray, sister of John of Strowan,

d) ADAM was Rector of Stobo in 1513,

e) HELEN married James Cunningham. They lived in Aiket, Scotland,

f) MARION married Colin Campbell. They lived in Ardkinlass, Scotland.

13) SIR JOHN 13TH OF COLQUHOUN AND 15TH OF LUSS was born 1515 and died about 1574. His service as Chief was from 1538 to 1574. He married first LADY CHRISTIAN ERSKINE, daughter of Lord Erskine and wife, Elizabeth Campbell, on Jan 25, 1535. She died without issue in 1564.

SIR JOHN 13th was knighted by Mary Queen of Scots who often visited Rossdhu, and is mentioned in the mysterious "Casket Letters",her alleged secret correspondence with Bothwell.

SIR JOHN 13TH signed his will May 20, 1564 and married second, LADY AGNES BOYD, daughter of Robert Boyd, 4th Lord Boyd, ancestor of the Earls of Kilmarnock. Agnes died in Edinburgh, Scotland and was buried there on July 18, 1584. Around the 1560's added greatly to the family possessions. Their children were all born in Dumbarton:

a) SIR HUMPHREY 14th Of COLQUHOUN AND 16TH OF LUSS,

b) JOHN ROY was born in 1567 and was beheaded at the Cross of Edinburgh on November 1, 1592. In the "Diary of Robert Birrell, the Burgess of Edinburgh" "Johnne Cachoune was beheided at the Cross of Edinburgh, for muthering of his ouen brother, the Lairde of Lusse" From CHIEFS OF COLQUHOUN (This was no doubt Humphrey 14th).

c) JEAN lived for a time in Minto, Scotland and then Glasgow. She married SIR MATTHEW STUART.

d) ALEXANDER was born 1573, married Helen Buchanan August 8, 1595 and died May, 23, 1617. He succeeded his brother, SIR HUMPHREY 14TH OF COLQUHOUN AND 16TH OF LUSS, as Chief of CLAN COLQUHOUN.

e) MARGARET married SIR JAMES EDMONSTONE, KNIGHT. They lived in Duntreath, Scotland.

During the rule of SIR JOHN 13th as Chief, Protestantism was formally established in 1547 . Edward VI was king. In 1553 Mary, Queen of Scots, was queen of England. In 1568, she took refuge in England and was captured by the English. She was executed in 1587. In 1554 Lady Jane Grey was executed.

SIR JOHN'S great grandson was made a Baronet of Nova Scotia in 1625. He abducted his sister-in-law, LADY KATHERINE GRAHAM, the daughter of the Earl of Montrose for which he was outlawed and excommunicated.

14) SIR HUMPHREY 14TH OF COLQUHOUN AND 16TH OF LUSS WAS BORN 1565. He serving as Chief from 1574-1592, acquired the heritable coronership of County of Dumbarton from Robert Graham of Knockdoclain, confirmed by charter in 1583. He married first on May 15, 1583 LADY JEAN CUNNINGHAM, daughter of Alexander Earl of Glencairn, widow of Archibald, 5th Earl of Argyll. She died before Jan 6, 1584.

He married second time on December 20, 1585 to LADY JEAN HAMILTON, daughter of Lord, John Hamilton 2nd son of Sir James Hamilton, Earl of Arran and Regent of Scotland for the infant queen, "Mary, Queen of Scots".

In 1592, SIR HUMPHREY 14th had a liaison with the MacFarlane Chief's wife. The enraged MacFarlanes surprised him at his dalliance and pursued him past Rossdhu to Bannachra, another of his castles, where they tried to smoke him out. In the ensuing confusion SIR HUMPHREY was slain by an arrow, apparently treacherously fired within the castle by his brother and heir, John Roy, who was executed for his crime and obviously did not receive the Chiefship as he had expected.

Their children all were born in Dumbarton:

a) JEAN in July, 1592 was ravished when their home at Bannachra was burned by a servant with a grievance. She died on December 25, 1593. Though he had slain the Chief and devastated the daughter, the COLQUHOUNS treated him and his family justly.

b) MARGARET lived in Glasgow as a single lady.

c) ANNA lived in Edinburgh , married Colin Campbell in 1610 and died there.

15)SIR ALEXANDER 15TH OF COLQUHOUN AND 17TH OF LUSS was born in 1573 and died May 23, 1617. He was born in Dumbarton, Scotland, had a grant of 1000 acres in Plantation of Ulster in county of Donegal, North Ireland, upon which by the grant he was required to make a residence upon the land for a period in each year. (See reference to e) below.)

It was during SIR ALEXANDER'S rule that the bloody battle of Glenfruin was fought resulting in cruelty and disaster to the COLQUHOUNS and the banishment of the MacGregors. Also, the island of Inchtavanich was granted to SIR ALEXANDER by MacAulay of Ardencaple. The island was planted many years before with yew trees under orders of KING ROBERT THE BRUCE to provide bows for the Scottish archers.

COLQUHOUN/CALHOUN

SIR ALEXANDER COLQUHOUN 15th married August 8. 1595 LADY HELEN BUCHANAN, daughter of SIR GEORGE of that ILK and died May 23, 1617. Beginning on January 11, 1592, he served as CHIEF OF CLAN COLQUHOUN as heir to his brother, SIR HUMPHREY 14TH. His will was signed on May 17, 1617. Their children were all born in Dumbarton:

a) SIR JOHN COLQUHOUN 16TH was born in 1596 and died in 1655 while in exile in Italy. He married first LADY LILIAS (Lillian) GRAHAM on July 6, 1620 and was made 1st Baronet of Nova Scotia.

b) HUMPHREY lived in Balvie, Scotland and married Margaret Somerville. He by his connections was able to save the family estates after his brother JOHN'S troubled times.

c) SIR ALEXANDER 17TH OF TULLICHEWAN married Marion Stirling in September 1631. Evidently his title as Chief came from the bride's side of the family. They had a daughter, Jean.

d) WALTER who lived and died in Sweden, received distinction as a cannon-founder. Many of his descendants still reside there under the surnames of Cahun, Cahund, Caun, Gaan, Gahn, and Kharun. Hugh Cahun, who was possibly Walter's son, revealed the conspiracy headed by Charles de Manay in September 1574, and lost his life in spite of a promise of pardon (Stodart, II p.

119). Other possible heirs were celebrated as heroes. Johan Gottlieb Gahn (1745-1818) was one of the greatest scientist of his day, and Henry Cahun Vulgo Gahn was physician to the Admiralty of Sweden in 1781.

e) ADAM was born in 1601 and died in December, 1634. He was expected to take the Title of Sir ADAM 16th but never accepted it. In 1621 he married LADY CHRISTIAN LINDSAY of Bonniel, Scotland. They lived in Dumbarton where he was a merchant. The property given to his father, SIR ALEXANDER COLQUHOUN 15TH, by grant in Corkagh County, Donegal, Northern Ireland required a family member to reside there for some part of each year. ADAM did this for his father and upon his death, ADAM inherited it by will in 1617. He in turn approved a transfer of title to his son ROBERT in 1630.

f) GEORGE entered Glasgow University on March 1, 1622. He went to Sweden to live and die there. He and his brother changed the family name to Cahun, Gahn, and other spellings.

g) JEAN married first LORD ALLAN CATHCART 5th BARON in 1626, second SIR DUNCAN CAMPBELL OF AUCHINBRECK, and third SIR WILLIAM HAMILTON, third son of James, the First Earl of Abercorn..

h) NANCY (Nans) lived in Corkagh Co., Donegal Ireland. She married John McAuselan.

i) KATHERINE lived in Maybole, Co. Ayr, Scotland, and married SIR JOHN MURE.

16) SIR JOHN 16TH OF COLQUHOUN AND 18TH OF LUSS served as Clan Chief from 1617 to 1647. He was born about 1596 and was named FIRST BARONET OF NOVA SCOTIA on Aug 30, 1625. He married LADY LILLIAS GRAHAM, eldest daughter of John 4th Earl of Montrose and sister of the 1st Marquis of Montrose who was a frequent visitor at Rossdhu. Their marriage contracts were dated June 30 and July 6, 1620. He fell in love with his wife's pretty sister, LADY KATHERINE GRAHAM. After eloping with her fled the country to die in exile in Italy. SIR JOHN was a necromancer who was skilled in Black Magic and was the last family member to openly practice witchcraft.

Their children:

a)SIR JOHN 17TH OF COLQUHOUN AND 19TH OF LUSS,

b)JAMES ALEXANDER COLQUHOUN OF TULLYCHEWEN, county of Dumbarton, Scotland married in 1664 Annabella Stewart, daughter of Archibald, brother of Sir Archibald Stewart of Black Hall, Baronet. Alexander died before 1676. The COLQUHOUNS OF TILLYQUHOUN descend from him.

c) JEAN married Walter Stewart in 1647.

COLQUHOUN/CALHOUN

d) LILLAS married John Napier, eldest son
of Robert of Kilmahew, county Dumbarton,
Scotland.

e) CATHERINE married John Drummond.

17) SIR JOHN 17TH OF COLQUHOUN AND 19TH OF
LUSS SECOND BARONET OF NOVA SCOTIA,
dubbed "The Blackcock of the West" because
of his swarthy and arrogant manner,
served as CHIEF OF CLAN COLQUHOUN from
1647 to 1676. His portrait at Rossdhu is
of unusual interest, as he is wearing his
red baronial robes edged with white fur
which was unique for this period. During
his rule Rossdhu Castle was twice occupied
by the English Cromwellians for a short
time.

He matriculated at Glasgow University
March 15, 1642, was elected Commissioner
for Dumbartonshire to the Convention of
the Estates, 1665, and served as Lt. Col
of Argyll Regiment of Militia. Marriage
contract was dated 2/17/1636 to Margaret
Baillie daughter of Lochend, Baronet of
county Haddington and wife, Magdalen
Carnegie, 2nd daughter of Lord David,
Margaret died July 20, 1679. Their
children were:

a) JOHN

b) SIR JAMES 18TH

18) SIR JAMES 18th OF COLQUHOUN AND 20TH OF LUSS, THE 3RD BARONET OF NOVA SCOTIA was in possession of Baronet title for only four years 1676-1680) serving while a minor. He was omitted from the family history until instruction by his father restored him to his rightful place in the family line. This was determined from papers found at Rossdhu. He was educated at Glasgow though did not complete the course prior to his death in Glasgow in April 1680. He was a single gentleman with great promise. At his demise notice was sent to his Uncle, JAMES COLQUHOUN of Belvie heir through his brother SIR JOHN 17TH OF COLQUHOUN AND 19TH OF LUSS, who was living in Ulster, Ireland in October of 1679.

19) SIR JAMES 19TH OF COLQUHOUN AND 21ST OF LUSS 4TH BARONET OF NOVA SCOTIA served as Chief of the Clan from 1680 TO 1688. He was brother of SIR JOHN 17TH OF COLQUHOUN AND 19TH OF LUSS. He married in 1659 Penuel Cunningham, one of the four daughters and co-heiress of William of Ballyachen, County Donegal, Ireland who was the son of Sir James Cunningham of Gengarnock county Ayr, Scotland and wife Lady Catherine daughter of James, Earl of Glencairn. Penuel died July 20, 1679 and SIR JAMES August 11, 1688. Their children:

a) SIR HUMPHREY 20TH OF COLQUHOUN AND 22ND OF LUSS,

44

b) JAMES (renounced his title and estate of Luss).

c) ELIZABETH married Alexander Falconer of Kepps, the second son of SIR JAMES OF PHEADO.

20) SIR HUMPHREY 20TH OF COLQUHOUN AND 22ND OF LUSS 5TH BARONET OF NOVA SCOTIA was Clan Chief from 1688 to 1718, and was married to Margaret Houstan, daughter of Patrick of that ILK. SIR HUMPHREY was a member of Parliament for Dumbartonshire in 1703. He died in 1718 and was buried in the open air chapel at Rossdhu. He opposed the Union but supported the Revolution Settlement of 1715. His Baronet title was recorded on contracts dated April 1 & 4, 1684. Their only child was ANNE COLQUHOUN, heiress of Luss from 1718 to 1724. She was born August 11, 1685 and died June 25, 1724. Her marriage to James Grant of Pluscardine was the first time the lineage passed through a female.

During SIR HUMPHREY 20TH'S tenure in 1707 and act of union of England and Scotland avowed a peaceful existence and the first united Parliament met. He was M. P. for Dumbartonshire in the last Scottish Parliament and voted against every Article of the Union. He resigned his Baronetcy to the crown and received a new patent, a legal agreement which involved the Chiefship in a kind of musical chairs. A son-in-law succeeded to the estate and resumed the name of Grant. The second son, SIR JAMES, continued the COLQUHOUN line.

21) JAMES GRANT OF PLUSCARDINE WAS 6TH BARONET OF NOVA SCOTIA. He was the 2nd son of Ludovic Grant of that Ilk. SIR HUMPHREY, who was born July 28, 1679 died in London, England Jan 16, 1747 thereby resigning his Baronetcy to Queen Anne for a new patent to himself in life rent, and his son-in-law and his heirs named therein in fee, but with the express limitation that he and his heirs so succeeding to that estate and title should be obligated to bear the name and arms of the COLQUHOUNS of LUSS. In 1718 the new Fair Maid of Luss, ANNE, inherited the vast estates of COLQUHOUN. SIR HUMPHREY 20TH OF COLQUHOUN AND 22nd OF LUSS was succeeded to his estate and honors by James Grant under the name and designation of "SIR JAMES COLQUHOUN OF LUSS" (For additional information see CLAN COLQUHOUN History.) Children by ANNE COLQUHOUN AND JAMES:

a) HUMPHREY was the eldest son and as HUMPHREY GRANT died unmarried in 1752.

b) SIR LUDOVICK BECAME 7TH BARONET

c) ALEXANDER was born September 8, 1709 and died March 12, 1712.

46

COLQUHOUN/CALHOUN

d) JAMES was born February 22, 1714 and
succeeded as SIR JAMES 23RD OF COLQUHOUN
AND 25TH OF LUSS.

e) FRANCIS was born Aug. 10, 1717. He
became a general in the army and married a
lady whose surname was Cox.

f) CHARLES CATHART was born April 3, 1723.

g) CAPTAIN R. N. COLQUHOUN,

h) JANET,

i) MARGARET,

j) ELIZABETH,

k) SOPHIA,

l) CLEMENTINE,

m) JEAN,

n) ANNE.

22) SIR LUDOVICK 22ND OF COLQUHOUN AND
24TH OF LUSS 7th BARONET OF NOVA SCOTIA
was Chief from 1719 to 1732. He succeeded
to the Grant Estates because his brother,
Humphrey, who was heir apparent, died
without issue. After SIR LUDOVICK's death
his brother SIR JAMES was proclaimed as
CHIEF OF CLAN COLQUHOUN.

23) SIR JAMES 23RD OF COLQUHOUN 25TH OF LUSS was 8TH BARONET OF NOVA SCOTIA AND 1ST BARONET OF BRITAIN from 1732 TO 1786. He was a highly civilized Chief though a warrior in his youth. He had been one of the earliest officers of the famous Black Watch and fought under King George II in person at the battle of Dettingen, the last battle which a British Sovereign commanded in the field.

He was born in 1714 and died in November of 1786, married April 12, 1740 to LADY HELEN SUTHERLAND who was born April 8, 1717 and died Jan. 7, 1791. She and her husband were both buried in the open air Rossdhu Chapel. She was the eldest daughter of Lord William of Strathnaver, who was the eldest son of John 19th Earl of Sutherland.

SIR JAMES in 1777 rebuilt the town on the Firth of Clyde and named it Helensburgh for his wife. This was originally Milligs but as houses were erected and industries established the name was changed to Helensburgh. Though the desire of SIR JAMES to have a thriving town of bonnet makers, stockings, linen and woollen weavers did not materialize, those whose wealth would allow, built large country homes with wide expanse of land surrounding them above the streets of the village.

Their children were:

a) SIR JAMES 24th CHIEF OF COLQUHOUN and 16th of LUSS was proclaimed Second Baronet,

b) WILLIAM married Elizabeth Henderson.

c) LUDOVICK was born July 25, 1757 and married Barbara Camilla the daughter of Rev. Dr. MacIntire.

d) CATHERINE married Sir Mackenzie the Baronet of Scatwell.

e) ANNE was born December 26, 1746 and died April 9, 1748.

f) JANET married in 1766 General John Campbell of Barbreck.

g) MARGARET married William Baillie of Polkemet and had a son, Sir William Baillie, Baronet.

h) HELEN married WILLIAM COLQUHOUN of Garscadden from County of Dumbarton, Scotland.

i) JANE married Evenezer Marsall Gardner, Hillcairiney County, Fife, Scotland.

24) SIR JAMES 24TH OF COLQUHOUN AND 26TH OF LUSS SECOND BRITISH BARONET was born July 28, 1741 and served as Chief from 1786 to 1805, was elected Sheriff-de-pute of Dumbartonshire, and as one of the principal clerks of Session in 1779. After his death at Edinburgh on April 23, 1805

at the age of 64 years, he was buried at Rossdhu Chapel. He married Mary Falconer of Monktown on July 12, 1773. She, the youngest daughter and co-heiress of James of Monktown, died at Annfield House, Fifeshire, Scotland on April 12, 1833.

SIR JAMES 24TH was a friend and correspondent of Horace Walpole, to whom he gave a goat's horn snuff-mull. Walpole was a connoisseur and collector of paintings, landscapes in particular, engravings, ancient coins and rare old china. These items began the collection of art for the home.

Before his reign as Chief in 1772, he began construction on the present mansion of Rossdhu, which was originally the central block, and completed it in the following year. LADY HELEN was very contented with her new home and entertained famous guests. Her policy was to see that nothing was wasted. Her ghost is reported to have been in the staff's quarters on several occasions. Sir James and Lady Helen's names are written on the roof of Rossdhu.

Their children were:

a) SIR JAMES 25th OF COLQUHOUN AND 27TH OF LUSS was third British Baronet.

b) WILLIAM died in infancy.

c) PATRICK died unmarried before November 25, 1805.

d) LUDOVICK died in infancy.

e) JOHN CAMPBELL was born January 31, 1785 and died August 21, 1854.

f) CORPORAL SUTHERLAND MORRISON, ROYAL NAVY, died unmarried in February 1827.

g) RODERICK, ROYAL NAVY, died unmarried at Edinburgh in 1834.

h) JANE married David Kemp of Belsumset Lodge, County Fife, Scotland.

i) HELENE lived at 10 Melville St., Edinburgh, 1877.

25) SIR JAMES 25TH OF COLQUHOUN AND 27TH OF LUSS 3RD BRITISH BARONET was baptized September 30, 1774 and was acting Clan Chief from 1805 to 1836. He was born in Edinburgh,Scotland and served Dumbarton as member of Parliament 1801, 1802-06. He died in Edinburgh Feb. 3, 1836, age 62 years and was buried in Rossdhu Chapel. His spouse by marriage contract dated in Edinburgh on June 11, 1799 was his cousin, Janet Sinclair of Ulbster who was born in London, England on April 17, 1781 and died Oct. 21, 1846 at age 62 years. Her days were spent with Christian works and writing of them. She also was buried in Rossdhu Chapel. A portrait of her father, SIR JOHN SINCLAIR in his usual uniform, is a copy of a famous Raeburn picture which

hung above the fireplace in the main hall of Rossdhu.

SIR JAMES 25TH OF COLQUHOUN AND 27TH OF LUSS lived with good taste during this choice period of his Regency. He enlarged the house, adding the two wings and the portico, using the stone from the old castle. The long south drive along the lochside was built as were two superb entrance lodges joined by a beautiful archway surmounted by the COLQUHOUN heraldic emblems, which form together an architectural gem on the side of the main road. He had the mossy ground that had guarded the landward side of the castle in the Middle Ages, now no longer needed, made into a deer park and enclosed the policies within a park wall. He was generous to his blood-feud foes, the Clan Gregor, whom he invited to Rossdhu with a ceremonial handshake between SIR JAMES and MacGregor on the overgrown site of the battlefield of Glenfruin. Such a scene could perhaps only have occurred in the romantic Scotland enlightened by their friend and contemporary Sir Walter Scott, who wrote the poem "The Lady of the Lake": Their children were :

a) SIR JAMES COLQUHOUN 26TH OF COLQUHOUN AND 28TH OF LUSS was 4th BRITISH BARONET.

b) JOHN, born February 7, 1805, married Frances Sarah Maitland the fourth daughter of Ebenezer Fuller, Esq. of Park Place, Henley. John was author of several books on sporting and wildlife. "The Moor and the Loch" was probably the most famous, which painted a picture of the country gentleman whose ardor was mastery of the hunt.

c) WILLIAM was born October 1, 1806 and married Sarah Maitland who was born August 8, 1802.

d) HELEN, born November 7, 1804, married John Page Reade of Sutton House, Ipswich on April 9, 1829. They had one son, John.

26) SIR JAMES 26TH OF COLQUHOUN AND 28TH OF LUSS 4TH BRITISH BARONET was Clan Chief from 1836 to 1873. He was born February 7, 1804, served as member of Parliament for Dumbarton in 1837, and as Lord Lieutenant of Dumbarton County. His lamentable death was by drowning in Loch Lomond just as they approached Rossdhu after hunting deer on the island. His boat capsized during a tempest and tossed him overboard causing his death.

He married on June 14, 1843 Jane Abercombie 2nd daughter of Sir Robert, Baronet of Birkenbob. She died May 3, 1844, leaving one son, SIR JAMES 27TH OF COLQUHOUN AND 29TH OF LUSS, born 1844.

SIR JAMES 26TH purchased Ardencaple on the bay between Helensburgh and Rhu in 1852. This was the homeplace of the MacAulays who customarily raided the property of Luss.

27) SIR JAMES 27TH OF COLQUHOUN AND 29TH OF LUSS 5TH BRITISH BARONET Clan Chief from 1873 to 1907 was born 1844 . He was visited at Rossdhu by Queen Victoria in 1875. He was educated at Harrow and Cambridge, and married first Mary Douglas. His second wife sold the family ancestral treasures which she inherited upon the death of her husband. Replacement of the original items was difficult but gradually over the years other Highland relics were purchased and placed in the home at Rossdhu.

28) SIR ALAN 28TH OF COLQUHOUN AND 30TH OF LUSS 6TH BRITISH BARONET- Chief of Clan from 1907 to 1910 was son of JOHN COLQUHOUN and Frances Sarah Maitland and cousin of SIR JAMES 27TH OF COLQUHOUN AND 30TH OF LUSS. SIR ALAN married Justine Henrietta Kennedy of Underwood. He was heir of uncle SIR JAMES 25TH OF COLQUHOUN AND 27TH OF LUSS.

Son: SIR IAIN COLQUHOUN.

29) SIR IAIN 29TH OF COLQUHOUN AND 31ST OF LUSS 7TH BRITISH BARONET was dubbed "Knight of the Thistle" and Grand Master Mason of Scotland, was elected by the students as their Lord Rector of Glasgow University, and was Chief from 1910 to his death in 1948. His marriage to Geraldine Bryde Tennant produced one son: Ivar.

He was lightweight boxing champion of the whole British Army, and became a Lt. Colonel in the Scots Guards. His exploits in the First World War are renowned, though he suffered a wound in the thigh by a German bullet when it struck his sword at the Battle of Ypres. His life was saved by placing green cowpats on the wound, a primitive penicillin ahead of its time. He was condemned to death by a court martial for fraternizing on Christmas Day with the Germans in No Man's Land in 1915 but was pardoned by King George V. Sir Iain who won the Distinguished Service Cross and Bar kept a fairly tame pet lion in the trenches.

He killed five Bavarians with an improvised club, and shot a Prussian officer at the very moment the Prussian's bullet hit his revolver's chamber and jammed it in his stunned hand. He thought it had been shot off until the end of the battle when he found it was still attached to his arm. His sword with its damaged guard, his club with five little death-nicks in its handle, and his revolver with one round fired and the rest jammed and sprayed with the lead of the German bullet, are all almost unbelievably still at Rossdhu for all to see.

SIR IAIN of all the long line of Chiefs was the most popular. His trim torso, a kilted figure was familiar in many places. In the Great War he was mentioned in dispatches five times and twice was wounded. Though he had the prestige of being Lord High Commissioner to the General Assembly of the Church of Scotland, the highest position in the country superceding that of the royalty and heir to the throne, he deserves especially to be remembered for his work for the preservation of his country's ancient monuments and scenery and his aid in encouragement of open air recreation. He did much to preserve the beauty of Loch Lomond.

Their son is SIR IVAR 30TH OF COLQUHOUN AND 32ND OF LUSS.

30) SIR IVAR 30TH OF COLQUHOUN AND 32ND OF LUSS 8TH BRITISH BARONET upon the death of his father assumed the title of Chief of Clan COLQUHOUN and is living today at Rossdhu in January, 1993. His spouse is Kathleen Duncan.

COLQUHOUN/CALHOUN

ROBERT COLQUHOUN RANDEL LINEAGE CHART

1) UMFRIDUS DE KILPATRICK AND DE COLQUHOUN 1190-1260

2) SIR ROBERT OF COLQUHOUN 1260-1280

3) INGELRAMUS DE COLQUHOUN 1280-1308

4) SIR HUMPHREY OF COLQUHOUN 1308-1330

5) SIR ROBERT 5TH OF COLQUHOUN AND OF 7TH LUSS 1330-1390 married the Heiress of Luss. Their children were:

a) SIR HUMPHREY 6TH OF COLQUHOUN AND 8TH OF LUSS,

b) ROBERT, FIRST LAIRD OF CAMSTRADDEN,

c) PATRICK.

(EXPLANATION OF THE FIVE CHIEFS ABOVE ARE LISTED ON COLQUHOUN CHART)

6) ROBERT COLQUHOUN, FIRST LAIRD OF CAMSTRADDEN. 1395-1439 obtained the estate of Achiagahan which was a portion of the estate of LUSS by charter dated July 4th 1395 from his brother, SIR HUMPHREY 6TH OF COLQUHOUN AND 8TH OF LUSS. SIR JAMES 24TH OF COLQUHOUN AND LUSS, SECOND BARONET purchased the estate and rejoined it to the COLQUHOUN/LUSS lands during his reign from 1786-1805.

ROBERT, FIRST LAIRD OF CAMSTRADDEN, second son of SIR ROBERT 5TH OF COLQUHOUN AND 7TH OF LUSS, married a daughter of Duncan More MacNaughton. He was a witness to a resignation made by John MacRoger to SIR JOHN THE 8TH OF COLQUHOUN AND 10TH OF LUSS, dated February 7th 1429. He died in 1439 and was succeeded by their son, JOHN.

7) JOHN COLQUHOUN, SECOND LAIRD OF CAMSTRADDEN 1439-1441 married Mary, daughter of Alex Galbraith of Culcrench. He died 1441 and was succeeded by their son ROBERT.

8) ROBERT COLQUHOUN, THIRD LAIRD OF CAMSTRADDEN 1441-1473, married Elizabeth, daughter of Robert Sempile of Fulwood. He died before 1473 and was succeeded by his son, JOHN.

9) JOHN COLQUHOUN, FOURTH LAIRD OF CAMSTRADDEN 1473-1503, SON OF ROBERT AND ELIZABETH, married Jean Maxwell. He died January 10, 1505 and was succeeded by his eldest son. ROBERT.

10) ROBERT COLQUHOUN, FIFTH LAIRD OF CAMSTRADDEN 1503-1525, married first wife, Christian, daughter of Walter MacFarlane. He was succeeded in 1529 by his and Christian's son, ROBERT.

COLQUHOUN/CALHOUN

11) ROBERT COLQUHOUN, SIXTH LAIRD OF
CAMSTRADDEN 1525-1530 married first
Elizabeth Cunningham and second Janet
Landes, daughter of "Leader of the Bass"
and was succeeded in 1530 by his son,
JOHN.

12) JOHN COLQUHOUN, SEVENTH LAIRD OF
CAMSTRADDEN 1530-1563 married his first
cousin, Christian, daughter of John
Lindsay of Bonhill, by MARGARET COLQUHOUN,
daughter of ROBERT, FIFTH LAIRD OF
CAMSTRADDEN. He died before June 1564 and
left a son, ROBERT.

JOHN COLQUHOUN'S second wife was MARGARET
COLQUHOUN, Daughter of ROBERT FIFTH LAIRD
OF CAMSTRADDEN.

13) ROBERT COLQUHOUN, 1563-1616 married
Mariota Murry. Their children were:

a) Patrick died Sine Paroles 1576,

b) JOHN, EIGHTH LAIRD OF CAMSTRADDEN and
ancestor of Killermonts, William of
Dunglas County, Dumbarton,

c) James,

d) Margaret,

14) JOHN, EIGHTH LAIRD OF CAMSTRADDEN,
1616-1642 fought at the battle of Pinkie
in 1547. After saving the life of William
Auchencrosh he was granted the lands of

Temphill in Kilpatrick and also obtained a lease of adjoining lands of Bochair from the Earl of Montrose. His daughter, Janet, married her cousin, John Dhu, son of ROBERT COLQUHOUN of CAMSTRADDEN. JOHN, EIGHTH LAIRD married Elizabeth, daughter of Robert Denzelestoun. His minor son, JOHN, succeeded him as Laird of Camstradden.

(ROBERT COLQUHOUN RANDEL'S LINEAGE PARTS HERE FROM THE REMAINING CAMSTRADDEN LINE. SEE #15 FOR CONTINUATION OF THIS CHART.)

1) ROBERT COLQUHOUN 1642-1669 son of JOHN and Elizabeth. ROBERT married first, Mary, daughter of Alex McCauley and second Janet Buchanan. He was succeeded by ALEXANDER COLQUHOUN.

2) ALEXANDER COLQUHOUN 1669-DIED 1699. He married first in 1644 Anne, daughter of John Graham; second Christian, daughter of ROBERT COLQUHOUN. Children of ALEXANDER AND CHRISTIAN were:

a) Walter,

b) Christian,

c) Janet.

Son of ALEXANDER AND FIRST WIFE, ANNE:

d) John

COLQUHOUN/CALHOUN

3) JOHN COLQUHOUN 1699-1717 married Margaret, daughter of John Tuill. Second Elizabeth in 1707. He was succeeded by sons, Robert & John. Robert married Jean Darleith Alexander.

4) JOHN COLQUHOUN, son of John and Elizabeth, born October 20, 1709 married Jean Taylor. He died before 1729. Their two sons were: LUDOVICK COLQUHOUN AND ROBERT COLQUHOUN.

5) ROBERT COLQUHOUN (ROBERT COLQUHOUN RANDEL'S LINEAGE). No family history is available on this ROBERT except that he had twin sons:
    Robert
    James (RCR's line)

6) JAMES COLQUHOUN married Martha (Patsey) Gatewood. He was succeeded by son, JAMES.

7) JAMES COLQUHOUN was born October 22, 1809 and died February 14, 1877. He married in Danville, VA on December 24, 1833 Mary Francis Sulivan who was born March 11, 1818 and died August 6, 1888. They had the following fifteen children as copied from COLQUHOUN Family Bible given to Mary Francis by her son, Walter COLQUHOUN, dated December 25, 1870:

James D. and Robert N. (twins) born June 14, 1830.

James D. died April 21, 1873
Robert N. died December 6, 1890
Christibell born October, 1834 died
November 1834
William H. Shelton born July 4, 1837 died
July 15th 1837
Janet born July 31, 1839 died November 9,
1870.
MARTHA ANN COLQUHOUN (MOTHER OF ROBERT
COLQUHOUN RANDEL) born January 30, 1841
died June 22, 1916
Emeline born February 8, 1843 died May 0,
1916
Walter born April 11, 1840 died August 23,
1916
Lucy Lee born April 25, 1848 died July
1858
Mary born August 1, 1844 died March ??
Estelle born April 3, 1850 died November
15, 1887
Clara Cleemans born January 11, 1852 died
May 8, 1912
Hortense born May 17, 1854 died March 19,
1878
Ludvic born March 11, 1856 died February
8, 1864
Sulivan born December, 1859, stillborn

8) MARTHA ANN COLQUHOUN married James
Mason RANDEL in Brandon, Mississippi on
July 12, 1863. Ceremony performed by Rev.
Drane. His father was from Kentucky and
his mother from Vermont. MARTHA ANN's
parents were both from Virginia. He died
January 30, 1902 and she died June 22,
1916 in Kansas City and was buried in
Canton, Mississippi. Their children were:

Mary Miranda Randel born October 25, 1864 died September 28, 1866
James Randel born July 28, 1866 died with pneumonia on May 14, 1884. He was born in Iowa
Walter Lee Randel born June 22, 1868 died August 16, 1929 in Kansas City, KS. He married Vinnie White on December 20, 1899. Their two children were Martha Ann Randel (Blum) and Thomas Randel
William Wallace Randel born July 1, 1871 died with TB April 10, 1897. He was born in Iowa
Estelle Randel (Wiggins & Gulledge) born September 29, 1873 died May 17, 1941. She was born in Iowa
ROBERT COLQUHOUN RANDEL (see 9)
Benjamin Randel born October 12, 1880 and died August 4, 1950. He married Katherine Merchant January 9, 1912

9) ROBERT COLQUHOUN RANDEL was born in Madison County, Mississippi on July 9, 1875 and died March 16, 1963. He married Laura Arabella Taylor on June 26, 1912 in Canton, Mississippi. She was born March 17, 1893 and died November 11, 1965 in Yazoo City, Mississippi. Their daughter, Ellen Swan Randel (Johnson), succeeds them.

10) ELLEN SWAN RANDEL (JOHNSON) was born May 9, 1916 and is living to write this book after her 76th birthday in 1992. She married Floyd Everett Johnson, Sr. He was

born in Jacoby, Louisiana on June 1, 1908. Their children:

a) DOLLY JOHNSON (DAY) born September 10, 1937. She married Larry Hale Day, MD on June 19, 1959. He was born August 30, 1937. They have three daughters:

    1) Sandra Lynn Day born May 18, 1961

    2) Lee Angela Day born June 1, 1962. She married Barry Neal Pinnix on March 7, 1987. They have one daughter, Laura Kristin Pinnix born April 28, 1989

    3) Laura Ellen Day born May 18, 1969

b) FLOYD EVERETT JOHNSON, JR. born February 28, 1941. He married Sandra Lee Huning Schneider on December 19, 1970. They have two daughters:

    1) Jennifer Lynn Johnson born June 14, 1973.

    2) Melinda Lee Johnson born March 5, 1975.

OTHER FACTS AND DATES FROM THIS COLQUHOUN LINE

MARRIAGES

Mary COLQUHOUN, daughter of James and Mary Francis COLQUHOUN of Canton, Mississippi, was wife of Charles C. Balfour.

COLQUHOUN/CALHOUN

Janet COLQUHOUN married Charles Clifton Balfour August 22, 1863 in Montgomery, Alabama.

Robert N. COLQUHOUN and Alice D. Latimer married December 5, 1865. Ceremony performed by Rev. G. Andrews.

Nan COLQUHOUN and C. E. Balfour married October 3rd 1870. Ceremony performed by Rev. M. Harris.

Walter COLQUHOUN and Sally Unthank married January 26, 1881.

Clara Cleemans COLQUHOUN and Samuel T. McKee married January 10, 1884 by Rev. W. L. C. Honnicut.

CHILDREN

Children of Charles C. COLQUHOUN and Janet Balfour:
1-James born 1865 and died 1865
2-Charles Clifton born May 8, 1867
3-Janet born December 17, 1869

Children of Robert N. COLQUHOUN and Alice Latimer:
1-Robert Latimer born January 20, 1868
2-Mary Ellen born December 18, 1870
3-James Daniel born July 31, 1873, died August, 16, 1875
4-Fannie born August 1876 died December 22, 1877
5-Rufus Neely born 1878
6-Alice born 1881

COLQUHOUN/CALHOUN

7-Walter Winchester born 1885

Children of Charles Clifton COLQUHOUN and Mary Balfour
1-Sallie COLQUHOUN born September 22, 1872
2-William L. born December 19, 1875 died September 4, 1882
3-James Roach born August 4, 1877

Children of Walter
COLQUHOUN and Sallie Unthank
1-Mary Bell born October 24, 1882
2-James born January 1885, died April 3, 1885
3-Walter Unthank born June 22, 1886 died 1937
4-Lizzie Neely born September 17, 1888 died July 28, 1889
5-Robert Walker born January 2, 1891
6-James Norman born January 4, 1897

66

COLQUHOUNS OF CAMSTRADDEN
Continued

*

15) JOHN COLQUHOUN, a minor at his father's death, was reportedly the first who was baptized into the Reformed Church in the Parish of Kilpatrick. He married Margaret daughter of Allanson of Blackwaline. Their children:

a) Daughter who married Lindsay of Little Tillechewan, nephew to the Laird of Bonhill.

b) John the elder son who was a merchant drowned in 1628 while crossing from Ireland.

c) WILLIAM COLQUHOUN, the second son who succeeded his father.

16) WILLIAM COLQUHOUN married Isabella, daughter of Patrick Lang of Netherclose, and had a son, WILLIAM, who succeeded him.

17) WILLIAM COLQUHOUN, was born in 1620, purchased in 1655 the five merkland of Garscadden and in 1660 the lands of Easter Ledecameroch of Ledecameroch Douglas. He married Agnes, daughter of Andrew Sterling of Law and died May 1666. His son Andrew succeeded him.

18) ANDREW COLQUHOUN of Garscadden was born 1654 was vested heir to his father October 2, 1675. In 1685 he and James Smollett were the commissioners to the Privy Council for Dumbartonshire. Marriage contracts dated May 26 and June 1, 1677 showed marriage of ANDREW to Jean, daughter of Hugh Crawford of Jordan Hill. Their children were:

a) Archibald

b) Hugh

c) John

d) William

19) James Patrick Calhoun born in Donegal, Ireland in 1694, came to America in 1733. Died in South Carolina in 1772. His wife, Catherine Montgomery, was born in Ireland in 1684 and was one of the twenty-three killed by the Indians near Long Cane Creek, South Carolina in 1760. Their children were:

a) Patrick, Jr., father of John C. Calhoun prominent statesman from South Carolina.

b) William

c) John

d) Ezekial

e) Catherine

f) James was born in Donegal, Ireland, 1723 and buried in Lebanon Cemetery in Pennsylvania

20) WILLIAM CALHOUN (see b above) married Agnes Long in October 1749. Their children were:

a) Joseph

b) Catherine was killed in an Indian raid in 1760

68

c) Ann married John Matthews. Their son Joseph Calhoun Matthews married Margaret Brown

d) Mary

e) Patrick was killed in an Indian raid in 1760

f) Rachel

g) Esther

h) William

i) Ezekial

j) Agnes

k) Alexander

21) JOSEPH CALHOUN MATTHEWS and Margaret Brown had the following children.

a) Ezekial

b) Nancy

c) Caroline

d) Rachel

e) Jane

f) Elizabeth

g) Mary

h) Thomas

69

CALHOUN/COLQUHOUN

i) Margaret

j) Lauren

k) Joseph

l) Lucretia

This family moved to Calhounville, near Atlanta, Georgia

22) JAMES CALHOUN, (see 19f) came to America with his father and family of children. JAMES died on February 14, 1799 and is buried in Allegheny County Pennsylvania in Lebanon Cemetery, Mifflin Township. He served in Revolutionary War as Lieutenant in Capt. James Caldwell's 6th Battalion and a Lieutenant Colonel under James Taylor's Lancaster County Militia Pennsylvania. His children were:

a) Matthew

b) James who died August 20, 1847 age 82

c) John Calhoun married Elizabeth Gardner, who died August 9, 1849, age 72. They had two children, James and Elizabeth both deceased. John died March 7, 1853 age 78

d) William Calhoun married Miss Irwin and moved to Kentucky. One of his sons was a captain on a Mississippi River Steamer.

e) Three daughters (N). One married James Alexander, another James Paiden, and another named Swert.

f) David Calhoun, Revolutionary War veteran, married Eleanor King. Their fourth child was James Calhoun. He married Betsey Carnaham. Their third child was John King Calhoun who married Martha McClelland. Their fourth child was Mary Belle Calhoun who married William McClelland Kerr. Their only child was Floyd King Kerr who married Goldie G. Stover. Their first child is William Martin Kerr.

* THIS INFORMATION WAS FROM WILLIAM MARTIN KERR VIA PRODIGY (ON LINE COMPUTER SYSTEM). This and part of the Camstradden lineage of ROBERT COLQUHOUN RANDEL was written by JOHN FRANKLIN CALHOUN in 1894. He was an attorney and state senator in Minnesota at the time the material was written. This is only a portion of one of the twenty original copies.

COLQUHOUN/CALHOUN

THE CHIEFS OF CLAN COLQUHOUN

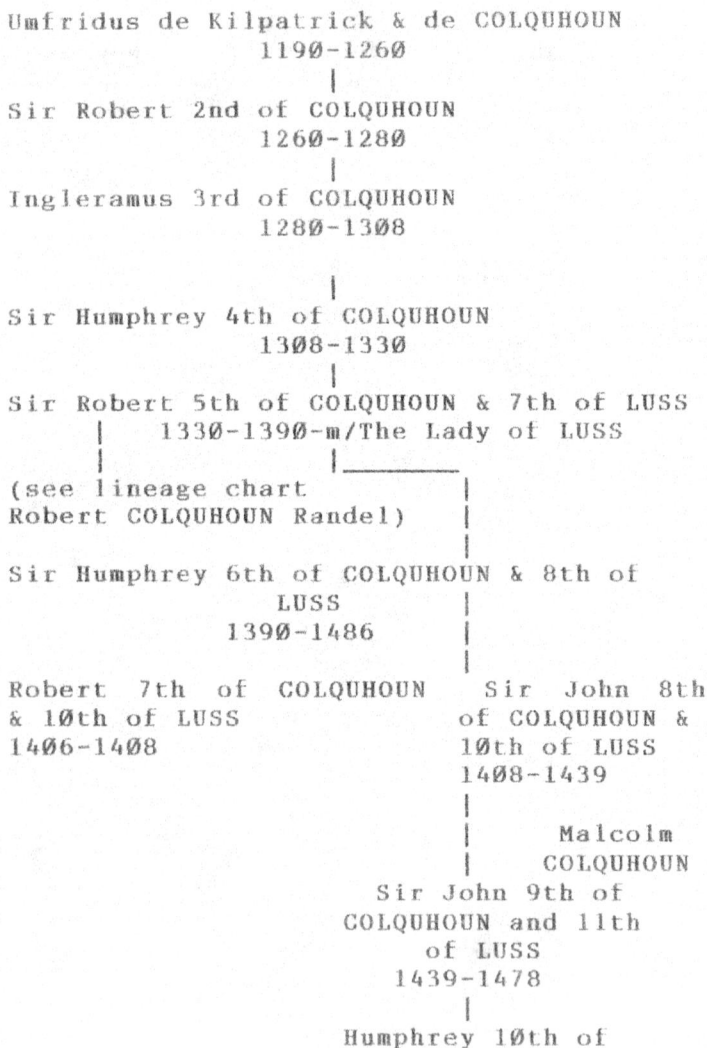

Umfridus de Kilpatrick & de COLQUHOUN
1190-1260
|
Sir Robert 2nd of COLQUHOUN
1260-1280
|
Ingleramus 3rd of COLQUHOUN
1280-1308

|
Sir Humphrey 4th of COLQUHOUN
1308-1330
|
Sir Robert 5th of COLQUHOUN & 7th of LUSS
| 1330-1390-m/The Lady of LUSS
| |_____
(see lineage chart |
Robert COLQUHOUN Randel) |
                          |
Sir Humphrey 6th of COLQUHOUN & 8th of
                LUSS |
              1390-1486 |
                          |
Robert 7th of COLQUHOUN   Sir John 8th
& 10th of LUSS   of COLQUHOUN &
1406-1408   10th of LUSS
                               1408-1439
                               |
                               | Malcolm
                               | COLQUHOUN
                      Sir John 9th of
                      COLQUHOUN and 11th
                         of LUSS
                       1439-1478
                          |
                  Humphrey 10th of

COLQUHOUN/CALHOUN

COLQUHOUN and 12th
of LUSS
1478-1493
|
Sir John 11th of
COLQUHOUN and 13th
of LUSS
1493-1536
|
Sir Humphrey 12th of
COLQUHOUN and 14th
of LUSS
Spouse: Lady Catherine
Graham, daughter of
Earl of Montrose
1536-1538
|
Sir John 13th of
COLQUHOUN and 15th
of LUSS
1538-1574
|

Sir Humphrey 14th   Alexander 15th of
of COLQUHOUN and   COLQUHOUN and 17th
16th of LUSS   of LUSS
1574-1592   1592-1617
|

Sir John 16th of
COLQUHOUN and 18th
of LUSS
First Baronet of
Nova Scotia
Spouse: Lady Lillias
Graham, sister of the
First Marquis of
Montrose
1617-1647
|

73

COLQUHOUN/CALHOUN

Sir John 17th of
COLQUHOUN and 19th
of LUSS
Second Baronet of
Nova Scotia
The Blackcock of
the West
1747-1676
|
Sir James 18th of
COLQUHOUN and 20th
of LUSS
Third Baronet of
Nova Scotia
1676-1680

Sir James 19th of
COLQUHOUN and 21st
of LUSS
Fourth Baronet of
Nova Scotia
1680-1688
|
|
|
|
|
|
|
|
Sir Humphrey 20th of
COLQUHOUN and 22nd
of LUSS
Fifth Baronet of
Nova Scotia
1688-1718
|
Anne, Heiress of
COLQUHOUN
1718-1724
|
James Grant of
Pluscardine- spouse
of Anne COLQUHOUN
He Sixth Baronet of
Nova Scotia
|

Sir   Ludovick   22nd
COLQUHOUN and
24th of LUSS
Succeeded to the
Grant Estates
Seventh Baronet

Sir   James   23rd   of
COLQUHOUN and 25th
of LUSS
Eighth Baronet of
Nova Scotia and
First Baronet of

COLQUHOUN/CALHOUN

Nova Scotia

Great Britain
Spouse: Lady Helen
Sutherland
1732-1786
|
Sir James 24th of
COLQUHOUN and 26th
of LUSS
Second Baronet of
Great Britain
Spouse: Mary Falconer
of Monktown
1786-1805
|
Sir James 25th of
COLQUHOUN and 27th
of LUSS
Third Baronet of
Great Britain
Spouse Janet Sinclair
of Ulbster
|
Sir James 26th of
COLQUHOUN and 28th
of LUSS
Fourth Baronet of
Great Britain
Spouse Jane Abercromie
Parents of John COLQUHOUN
Spouse Frances Sarah
Maitland.He author of "The
Moor and the Loch"
1836-1873
|
Sir James 27th   Sir Alan 28th of
of COLQUHOUN and   COLQUHOUN and 30th
28th of LUSS   of LUSS
                            Sixth Baronet of

Fifth Baronet of
Great Britain
1873-1907

Great Britain
Spouse Justine
Henrietta Kennedy
of Underwood
|
Sir Iain 29th of
COLQUHOUN and 31st
of LUSS
Seventh Baronet of
Great Britain
Knight of the Thistle
Spouse Geraldine
Bryde Tennant
1910-1948
|
Sir Ivar 30th of
COLQUHOUN and 32nd
of LUSS
Eighth Baronet of
Great Britain
Spouse Kathleen Duncan

BATTLES OF GLENFINLAS AND GLENFRUIN

(From the 1830 Edition of "Lady of the
Lake" by Sir Walter Scott, Canto Second XX
written in 1810)

"Proudly our pibroch has thrill'd in Glen
Fruin,
And Bannochar's groans to our slogan
replied;
GLEN LUSS AND ROSS-DHU, they are smoking
in ruin,
And the best of Loch Lomond lies dead on
her side.
Widow and Saxon maid
Long shall lament our raid,
Think of Clan-Alpine with fear and with
woe;
Lennox and Leven-glen
Shake when they hear again,
'Roderigh Vich Alpine dhu, ho! ieroe!'
Row, vassals, row for the pride of the
Highlands!
Stretch to your oars, for the ever-green
Pine!
O! that the rose-bud that graces yon
islands,
Were wreathed in a garland around him to
twine.
O, that some seedling gem,
Worthy such noble stem,
Honor'd and blessed in their shadow might
grow!
Loud should Clan-Alpine then Ring from her
deepest glen,
"Roderigh Vich Alpine dhu, ho! ieroe!"

Pibroch means music. Variations for the Scottish Highland bagpipe are usually martial or mournful. Clan-Alpine dhu for literary purposes referred to CLAN COLQUHOUN. Glen Luss was the land which once belonged to the old Earls of Lennox before acquisition by the COLQUHOUNS. This boat song was composed to honor a favorite chief. Boat songs are so adapted as to keep time with the sweep of the oars, and it is easy to distinguish between those intended to be sung to the oars of a galley, where the stroke is lengthened and doubled, and those which were timed to the rowers of an ordinary boat.

From the earliest days these men were warriors very nearly barbaric in temperament. The MacGregors and COLQUHOUNS were belligerent towards each other for many years causing terror to their neighbors and families. A petition to King James by SIR ALEXANDER COLQUHOUN resulted in permission being given to their Clan to carry arms and for them to wear various kinds of offensive weapons. This had enraged the MacGregors and in fact, stimulated their hatred for the COLQUHOUNS.

The earlier battle took place on the 7th of December in 1602 at Glenfinlas which was about two miles to the west of Rossdhu and three to the north of Glenfruin. Led by Duncan MacGregor the raiders plundered forty-five houses and killed two of the COLQUHOUNS. Then King James, sympathetic to the COLQUHOUNS, granted a commission of Lieutenant to ALEXANDER COLQUHOUN OF LUSS giving him power to stop the crimes perpetrated against his people and to apprehend and punish the MacGregors.

The feud had been too long and Alastair of Glenstrae, the Chief of MacGregors was determined in 1602 to put an end to it. He went to Luss accompanied by two hundred of his clansmen and friends to negotiate a settlement of their grievances.

Apparently the meeting was amicable and Alastair and his friends left for home at Rannach feeling that the matter was settled but still wary of the tricky COLQUHOUNS. SIR ALEXANDER quickly gathered a body of three hundred of his followers on foot and five hundred horsemen. Pursuing the MacGregors where no road led through a valley at Glenfruin often called the Glen of Sorrows, he attacked them. Though Alastair was confident the feud was ended, he feared some betrayal. With his men divided into two divisions, his brother, Iain Dubh, circled Auchinvennal Hill assaulting the COLQUHOUNS in the rear. He fought them with vehemence successfully routing the COLQUHOUNS who were caught in a trap in swampy ground on the Moss of Auchingaich where their horses bogged down.

They were easily defeated with some 200 COLQUHOUNS slain though the Chief escaped from his fallen horse and jumped across a wide stream only to be slain in the castle where he had taken refuge. Many of the MacGregors were wounded. The brother of the Chief, Iainglas, and another were the only ones who died in battle.

Many of the learned men of Dumbarton were spectators for the event in Glenfruin due only to curiosity. Some of them died at the hands of the MacGregors thus inciting the entire populace against them. Then the COLQUHOUNS prayed to the King to punish the MacGregors. Besides their petition, sixty widows on white ponies, and dressed in widow's weeds proceeded to the King's court. With much weeping and melancholy expression, they carried poles with two hundred twenty bloody shirts, and offered them to the King, loudly protesting the slaying of their loved ones. King James VI naturally opposed violent behavior, and, being sympathetic to the widows and their families, proscribed the whole race of MacGregor so thoroughly that they were crushed and not allowed to mistreat the COLQUHOUNS again.

Another version told by friends or foe said that since the COLQUHOUN lands were on the natural route between the Highlands and the Lowlands where Glenfruin road rejoined the Loch Lomondside highway at the policies of Rossdhu, the black point, home of the CHIEF OF THE CLAN, they had been molested by their neighbors, especially the MacGregors who lived across the Loch from them. In 1602 the COLQUHOUNS were given a royal commission by King James 6TH, son of Mary, Queen of

Scots, to lure the MacGregors into a trap and annihilate them. The MacGregors, hearing of the scheme, prepared to do battle with the COLQUHOUNS. This account stated that three hundred MacGregors bested CHIEF COLQUHOUN and seven hundred of his men, chasing the CHIEF home and storming his castle, Rossdhu. Within the six foot thick walls he took refuge.

The King was so furious that his plan had failed that when the widows appeared in his court, he outlawed the McGregors not allowing them to used their own name. One can hear the pipes play today "Ruaig Ghlinnefreoine" a lament tune that in English means "The Rout of Glenfruin".

Sir Walter Scott wrote many literary works and was instrumental in developing the form and shape of the novel. One of his most notable works is "Rob Roy" written in 1817. In his introduction to Rob Roy, Sir Walter puts the blame of beginning the feud upon the COLQUHOUNS. His narrative begins, "Two of the MacGregors, being benighted, asked shelter in a house belonging to a dependent of the COLQUHOUNS, and were refused. They then retired to an outhouse, took a wedder from the fold, killed it, and supped off the carcase, for which they offered payment to the owner. The LAIRD OF LUSS, however, unwilling to be appeased by the offer made to his tenant, seized the offenders, and by the summary process which feudal barons had at their command, caused them to be condemned and executed. The MacGregors verified this account of the feud by appealing to the proverb current among them, cursing the hour when the black wedder with the white tail was ever lambed."

Scott told a fictional tale about Rob Roy which painted him as a brute. A leader said he once was a follower of Rob Roy MacGregor who thought it was the proper time to make a raid on the lower part of the Loch Lomond district. Roy summoned all the heritors and farmers to meet at the Kirk of Drymen, to pay him black-mail (a tribute for forbearance and protection). As this invitation was supported by a band of thirty or forty stout fellows, only one gentleman, an ancestor of Mr. Grahame of Gartmore, ventured to decline compliance. Rob Roy instantly swept his land of all he could drive away, Among the spoils was a bull of the old Scottish wild breed, whose ferocity occasionally had plagued them all. (FROM: 1830 edition of footnotes from "Lady of the Lake") by Sir Walter Scott.

Another record of the Glenfruin conflict was told that the MacGregors were instigated to attack the COLQUHOUNS by Archibald, Earl of Argyll, who had his own ends to serve by bringing trouble on both clans. As a result of the constant raids by the MacGregors, SIR ALEXANDER COLQUHOUN in 1602 obtained a license from James 6TH to arm his clan. On the 7th of following February the two clans, each some three hundred strong, came face to face in battle array in Glenfruin. The battle was

so much a set affair that Alastair
MacGregor divided his force into two
parties, he himself attacking the
COLQUHOUNS in front, while his brother
John came upon them in the rear. The
COLQUHOUNS defended themselves bravely,
killing among others this John MacGregor;
but, assailed on two sides, they were at
last forced to give up. They were pursued
to the gates of Rossdhu itself, and one
hundred forty of them were slain,
including several near kinsmen of the
Chief and a number of burgesses of
Dumbarton who had taken arms in his cause.

According to a well-known tradition, some
forty students and other Dumbarton folk
had come up to witness the battle. As a
watch and guard MacGregor had set one of
his clansmen, Dugald Ciar Mhor, over these
spectators. On the COLQUHOUNS being
overthrown, MacGregor noticed Dugald join
in the pursuit, and asked him what he had
done with the young men. The clansman
held up his bloody dirk, and answered "Ask
that!"

The MacGregors followed up the defeat of
the COLQUHOUNS by plundering and
destroying the whole estate. They drove
off 600 cattle, 800 sheep and goats, and
14 score horses, and burned every house
and barnyard destroying the "Haill
plenishing, guids, and gear of the four
score pound land of Luss" while the
unfortunate chief, SIR ALEXANDER
COLQUHOUN, looked on helpless from within
the walls of the old castle of Rossdhu,

the ruins of which still stand on the rising grounds behind the modern mansion.

Then the story of the sixty widows in deep mourning again is repeated with little variation except that it was suggested that this parade was not all genuine; that these women were not all widows, and that the blood on the shirts had not been shed in Glenfruin. But King James 6th not liking the look and smell of blood denounced the MacGregors, stating that if anyone sheltered one of the clan it was a crime punishable by death.

While his men were hunted with dogs along the hills, the chief, Alastair Gregor, was enticed across the border by the promise of his false friend, Argyll. The latter had given his word that he would see him safely into England, since King James 6th of Scotland and I of England, had removed his court. No sooner was MacGregor across the border than Argyll had him arrested and carried back to Edinburgh, where, with four of his henchmen, he was tried, condemned, and hanged at the Cross, while all his possessions were declared forfeited.

Sir Walter Scott's version some two hundred years after the Battle of Glenfruin took place differs little from the legendary story told by the COLQUHOUNS. It is said, that Sir Walter had been treated with somewhat scant courtesy on the occasion of a visit which he paid to the residence of the COLQUHOUN Chief.

The ultimate result of the battle was very different from what might have been expected. While the MacGregors were hunted and harried through all their raids, the COLQUHOUNS quietly settled again on their lovely loch shore. Their subsequent fortunes illustrated well the old saying "Happy is the nation that has no history."

LIFE IN THE MIDDLE AGES

After the death in 1542 of James 5th, Scotland was ruled by his widow, Mary of Guise, as regent for her young daughter, MARY, QUEEN OF SCOTS. QUEEN MARY was also the legal heir to Elizabeth of England's throne. She was the granddaughter of Henry 8th's sister, Margaret Tudor, who married James 4th of Scotland.

QUEEN MARY, when an adult, visited Rossdhu on several occasions with the primary purpose of playing golf with the COLQUHOUNS. Her life was entwined in the life of the COLQUHOUNS many times since they lived nearby and were a well-established Clan with the ability to take sides with the QUEEN in her time of troubles.

The story was told of an infant's coffin walled up close to the room where she gave birth to her son JAMES, future King of Scotland and England born June 19, 1566. Speculation was that the real heir to the throne was stillborn and quietly sealed in the wall of the castle. This body was discovered by workmen in 1830 when a hollow sound in the wall was found. This when opened contained an infant's body covered with a shroud and impressed with the letter I. The question that was then asked, "Who is this child?"

MARY, QUEEN OF SCOTS married Henry, Lord Darnley of Lennox on July 29, 1565. She was described as being irritable,

conceited, and daft, but she was the
QUEEN. After the birth of her son, JAMES
6TH, she vowed to DARNLEY, the acting
KING "My Lord, God has given me and you a
son begotten by none but you...here I
protest to God, as I shall answer to Him
at the great day of Judgement, this is
your son and no other man's."

That oath was given to establish JAMES 6TH
as her natural legitimate heir to
guarantee his succession to the
throne.This would preclude KING DARNLEY
from ascendancy to the kingship upon her
death. It had been long rumored that
David Rizzio, MARY's Italian secretary,
was the father of her child. DARNELY's
jealousy was suspected of being a motive
for the brutal stabbing of Rizzio.

DARNLEY was arrogant, impetuous and
morally worthless. Though MARY enticed
him with titles and trinkets, she soon
realized they had nothing in common and
excluded him from any real power and regal
authority at her court in Holyroodhouse.
Neither DARNLEY nor MARY were faithful to
their marriage vows.

DARNLEY's death was mysterious when his
body was found without any mark of the
enormous explosion which leveled the house
where he was recuperating following an
severe illness. He had been strangled.
Some said that his problem was smallpox
and others syphillis. Though he was not
popular with the citizenry, his death

remains one of the long lasting puzzles of Scottish history.

Though supposition that another woman, the Countess of Mar, was the true mother of the infant James 6th, it was dispelled when a serious illness that inflicted Mary began to appear in James 6th. This inherited disease of metabolism left James with recurrent abdominal colic, with prostration, nausea, vomiting and diarrhea, fits of unconsciousness, passage of urine resembling port wine in color, weakness and loss of function in the arms and legs, and dermatitis. These symptoms were typical of MARY's illness. Hereditary by nature this disease was prevalent into the 18th century and reportedly caused madness in GEORGE III.

Though rumors have not been put aside completely, the facial likeness to HENRY, LORD DARNLEY tends to dispel any idea that JAMES was illegitimate. The identity of the baby in the wall is still unknown.

MARY's marriage to Bothwell was an escape which she mildly protested when he abducted her to Dunbar Castle on April 23,1567. Rumors of their romantic interests were substantiated by secret letters that they were lovers before DARNLEY died. They married on May 15, 1567, and parted forever on June 15 of the same year after rebellious forces stormed the Borthwick Castle where Bothwell and MARY were living.

She was forced to abdicate her throne in
1567 due to her persecutions of the
Christians in Scotland. Her Catholicism
created many religious and political
conflicts among the Scots. She fled to
England where she was imprisoned and
later executed by Elizabeth I.

Picture a remote country disturbed by
unrest and assassination. Courtiers wrote
lyrical poetry, merchants traded and
amassed wealth, and the peasants sowed and
reaped, at first for the church and later
for the nobility. Women sat at their
spinning wheels while their husbands were
killed in Clan feuds. At court, assassins
wore rich velvets imported from abroad,
while far away in remote villages wolves
threatened family lives. The constant
wars between the nobles kept the King's
power weak. MARY, QUEEN OF SCOTS had been
constantly involved in pitched battles
with various factions of the nobility.

The Scottish warriors filled their days
during the middle ages until the 18th
century with making war and preparing
battle strategy for the Scots. The
Lowlanders, fearing daily for their life
from the struggles against the invading
Highlanders from the north and the
belligerent English soldiers from the
south, were more peaceful and spent much
of their time in farming and plying their
trades. Some grain, peas and beans were
grown by tilling the soil with a simple
handmade plow. Their divergent languages

made communication between them virtually
impossible.

The upper class was allowed the privilege
of living in castles built on top of a
hill so troops advancing toward their
homes could be spotted and preparations
could be made for the battles that were
sure to come. Clanspeople, Lairds,
friends and servants were summoned to join
in the fray with thoughts of fighting to
the death if need be to defend their
homes.

Rich Scotsmen rode in carriages pulled by
the finest horses while the poor eked out
a meager existence plodding in mud and
living in abject poverty. Disease was
rampant among them since sanitation
methods were primitive with animals
sharing the muddy streets and their homes.
Cholera, typhus, and other deadly diseases
affected them as many citizens died from
the contaminated environment.

Even the homes of the moderately well-to-
do tenant farmers were not good
healthwise. Their cottages had walls of
wattle and daub, or rough fieldstones with
no windows for ventilation and thatched
roofs held in place by ropes of twisted
heather. They were weighted down with
rocks for protection from the wind and
rain. The dirt floors made living
conditions unsafe for human habitation.
With no fireplace for heat and cooking
space, a make-do stove was built on the
earthen floor in a small room shared by

the entire family. Their beds and subsistence were constantly in the gloom of smoke and steam with only doors for outside air. Though considered barbarous, perhaps to those migrants who had been living in the hills and plains for centuries this was an acceptable life in a palace of sorts.

While life was hard for many, Highland children with homes in the quiet country were privileged to grow up during their younger days at play running in the heather topped fields with hair flying in the wind. Subjects of school days taught by fathers, mothers, grannies, uncles and aunts provided an education envied by many. The girls learned at an early age knitting, and baking to win a prize at the "bring and buy sales".

During the summer with their mothers' assistance, children prepared provisions for the family table for the coming icy weather of winter. Jams and jellies were made from the ripe fruit they picked while fighting off the bees and wasps at the same time.

Young boys learned to plow the ground, sow the seed and harvest the crops for their families and for their animals. Tending of the cattle, the pets, and household chores taught them the joys of working. Even the tiny tots began to work their gardens learning the difference between weeds and genuine organic plants needed for food and forage.

Not all life was work. The holidays began at Christmas time with tales of the "Goblins 'n' Turnips 'n' All Hallow's Eve." This story was told them each year generation after generation until it became well entrenched in their minds and hearts for all time. "Before the arrival of Christianity in the Celtic calendar we find that October 31 is the eve of the beginning of Winter and November 6 is New Year's Day! For, in the Celtic view, darkness comes before light, night gives birth to day, summer grows out of winter, so the year begins with winter - the half-dark."

Thus, in the Celtic New Year in the half-dark, people were allowed to communicate with the nether world. The dead could return to what had been their earthly homes, thus many of the New Year rituals called "the Hogmanay" focused on the need to provide nourishment for their ancestors. Food for the dead was put out on the porch with much ritual. Gates and windows were left unlocked to allow free passage for them. Witches were working spells on those nights as the populace carved faces on turnips to guard the doors of their homes. This custom grew into communal gatherings of Highlanders with meals of typical Celtic foods such as found in a separate chapter entitled "Scottish Table Fare".

An old rhyme which used to be recited by
groups of children on the doorstep is as
follows:

Rise   up!   Guid   wife,   and   shak'   yer
feathers,
And dinna think that we are beggars,
We are bairns come out to play
Rise up! and gle's oor Hogmanay.

The day will come when ye'll be deid
Ye'll neither care for meal or breid,
Rise up! guid wife and dinna spare
Ye'll hae less, we'll hae mair.
Up stocks, doon stools!
Dinna think that we are fules,
We are bairns come out to play,
Rise up! and gul's oor Hogmanay.

This   festivity   began   in   pre-Christian
times when Northern invaders brought it to
Scotland   from   Scandinavia.   One   large
burning   candle   with   six   smaller   candles
circling   it   chased   the   dark   as   the
participants   went   through   a   traditional
ritual which lasted until nearly midnight.
While joining hands the glorious Scottish
song "Auld Lang Syne" was sung.   Then the
age-old   Celtic   custom   of   kissing   and
partaking of a "wee dram" began.   When the
ceremony was over and everyone felt no
pain, they went to the door to find the
half-eaten food left for their dead.   They
would never know who came back to eat and
had gone his way again- never making his
visit known!!!

It is not clear whether the celebration of "Little Christmas" is the same as the Hogmanay. "Little Christmas" was celebrated on January 6th before the 11 days were removed from the year by the Julian calendar. In modern times the Hogmanay season seems to refer to the Yule season or the entire period from December 24th to January 6th.

There was a period in Scottish history when the celebration of Christmas and Hogmanay were outlawed. The bakers were required to turn in the names of people who purchased Yule bread so that they could be brought up on charges before the church. This caused the celebrations to be moved into the homes.

Retribution was severe and cruel for those who had committed a crime against the King. His laws were punishable by torture, fitted into the stockade, or put to death depending upon the severity of the offense. Women and children were exempt except if they were witches or murderers. In mid-1500s, witchcraft was so rampant that when witches were discovered they were not allowed to eat or drink water. Rest was restricted until they were legally tortured and a confession was made. After conviction, burning or drowning was their doom.

SIR JOHN 13th OF COLQUHOUN CLAN was a dabbler in the Black Arts, yet despite or because of this he was created a Baronet of Nova Scotia in 1625 by Charles I. He

married the eldest sister of Marquis of
Montrose, Lillias Graham, winning the
King's favor by being a devoted loyalist
in the Civil War. Oliver Cromwell
considered this an act not acceptable and
fined him 2000 pounds.

SIR JOHN then eloped with a younger sister
of the Marquis of Montrose, Lady Catherine
Graham who had taken refuge at Rossdhu.
He was accused of using his Black Art to
entice her, having used witches and
sorcerers. Thomas Carlippis, one of his
ordinary servants, was his assistant in
using against her certain jewels of gold
set with divers diamonds, rubies, and
other precious stones. From this fact one
may doubt whether there was much
necromancy after all in his winning the
hand of the fair young lady.

The dapper young baronet was
disenfranchised and excommunicated. With
his extravagance of her love-jewels, his
fines and extravagances, he lost his
property. Whether he was beheaded for his
acts or exiled to avoid punishment has
not been recorded. With many complications
and expert bargaining, their property was
recovered by his brother, SIR HUMPHREY
COLQUHOUN.

The male line of the COLQUHOUNS came to an
end with SIR HUMPHREY upon his death in
1715. His only daughter, Anne, married
James Grant of Pluscardine. SIR HUMPHREY
was the second son of Alexander. So for
the first time the transfer of title and

estates was passed through a female. (Complete account in CLAN COLQUHOUN HISTORY)

In 1847, when QUEEN VICTORIA visited Dumbarton Castle, she was received by SIR JAMES COLQUHOUN 26th as Lord Lieutenant. The carriage that she rode in to and from the landing place is still in the coach house at Rossdhu.

This SIR JAMES twenty-six years later was the sad victim of a December 18th tragedy. He was returning to Rossdhu with Christmas fare for his family and friends when his loaded boat capsized in a fierce storm within sight of his home. He and his friends were drowned.

Non-payment of taxes was punishable by imprisonment. Poll money was collected according to social rank. The higher the rank the higher the levy. Also, during the 16th century salt was smuggled into the country to avoid paying tax which was assessed to those who were fortunate enough to own it. By 1693 the assessments had been increased by adding tax upon tax so much so that they became a burden to all but the most wealthy.

Personal contacts with people of all ages taught character and a toughness of spirit to dispel the hardships that were imposed by their fellow Scotsmen, both friend and enemy. Their perpetual courageous spirit made them strong for generation after generation.

Not all about Scottish life was doom and sadness in the Middle Ages. Some contend that golf as is known today was initially a game of the gentlemen of Scotland. "Goff or gowf" in 1445 was outlawed by King JAMES 2ND because he thought it would interfere with their archery practice. Arrows shot from bows were used to protect the kingdom. However, MARY, QUEEN OF SCOTS played frequently on the courses at Rossdhu during her travels in Scotland. This sport was the beginning of the Scottish games, the festive days as we know them today. Caddies were first used during this time to carry clubs for the players. The avid golfers of modern times appreciate the Scots for the introduction of this pleasurable game of sport.

The Finglas Water flows into Loch Lomond through the lands of Rossdhu. Glenfinglas, the scene of the Macgregor raid in 1602-03, is described in the chapter "Battles Glenfinglas and Glenfruin. Two knolls by the roadside were from olden days the seat of justice and the gallows tree of the COLQUHOUNS. Further north, Cnoc Ealeachan, knoll of the willows was the gathering place of the COLQUHOUNS from which they acquired their slogan.

About a mile south of LUSS is Bandry where a landmark which was lost in the road widening was said to mark the place where St. Kessog, titular saint of the parish, was martyred in the 6th century AD. An effigy, believed to be of this saint, is now in the private chapel at Rossdhu. Saint Kessog as the legend goes had a small cell at Inchtavanich.

On top of a high hill there was a bell which in later centuries summoned the people to prayer. The island was granted in 1613 to SIR ALEXANDER COLQUHOUN 15th by MacAulay of Ardencaple. In the 18th century one family lived on this island. They boarded persons that had been addicted to drinking.

Inchlonaig island had been planted with yew trees many years before upon orders from KING ROBERT THE BRUCE to provide bows for the Scottish archers who were expert marksmen. SIR JAMES once met Rob Roy MacGregor there on the island.

Picturesque woods and streams provided hiding places for the fowl and animals that placed food on the table of the nobility and sport for them as hunters and fishermen as well. Notable among the hunters was John COLQUHOUN, author of "The Moor and the Loch" and other books on wildlife and the art of hunting.

The eccentricity of the residents of Scotland in the 18th century provided many laughs for antidotes recorded and told over and over again. One such story in 1714-99 tells that a certain gentleman hired a sedan-chair to take his wig home when it rained, while he ran alongside. Notorious for his odd behavior was Jamie

Duff who entered a horse race as a runner. He ran the course barefooted and half-bent over as a jockey would do, while whipping himself with a switch.

All people with strange behavior were dubbed Jamie Duffs. Whenever there was a large neighborhood of people usually there were those who were called "dafties". In those days they were cared for by their families who gave them whatever work they were able to perform. As institutions that were capable of caring for these distressed people were established, the Jamie Duffs gradually disappeared until soon there were no more.

The following poem penned by the renowned Scottish poet, Robert Burns, describes the end of a year and beginning of another.

"MIST"

The lazy mist hangs from the brow of the hill,
Concealing the course of the dark winding rill.
How languid the scenes, late so sprightly appear,
As Autumn to Winter resigns the pale year!
The forests are leafless, the meadows are brown,
And all the gay foppery of summer is flown.
Apart let me wander, apart let me muse,
How quick TIME is flying, how keen FATE pursues!

ROSSDHU

**

On the west bank of Loch Lomond is Rossdhu, the beautiful home of CLAN COLQUHOUN. They shared this bank with the MacFarlanes. On the right bank lived the MacGregors, Grahams and Buchanans, while the south bank was the home of the Cunninghams.

A special greeting is tendered to members of CLAN COLQUHOUN from all parts of the world to Rossdhu, the Gaelic term for "Black Headland". A pillared gateway with armorial design leads onto the ground of Rossdhu where the elegant Georgian house built in 1772 by SIR JAMES 23RD OF COLQUHOUN AND 25TH OF LUSS stands adjacent to the ruins of the mediaeval castle and a roofless chapel which dates back to the 12th century where generations of Chiefs are buried. This destruction was by warring men.

Though the road was not carved out of the rocky hillside until more peaceful times, neighbors were constantly aggravating the COLQUHOUNS. The MacFarlanes had carried off in 1592 the gates of Rossdhu and erected them at Tighvechtan, the house of the watch, near Tarbet.. This "come and get them" gesture was not one to be ignored by the COLQUHOUNS. Led by SIR ALEXANDER, they made their way north by the String of Luss and descended on Tarbet. The chief of the MacFarlanes was drinking in an inn but managed to escape by a rear window and assemble his men. The

COLQUHOUNS, outnumbered, were forced into retreat. Time and good fortune were on the side of the COLQUHOUNS whose lands and the estate extend up the Loch and into the ancient territory of their old foes.

From earliest recorded accounts of the forefathers all charters mention COLQUHOUN family members. Before the written records all was marsh and primeval forest and uncultivated with no roads but with bloodstained turf of their family and their enemies.

The COLQUHOUN of LUSS coat-of arms resembles that of the Earls of Lennox from whom they obtained the land. Many relics saved from the early times were sold by SIR JAMES 23rd CHIEF's second wife. Rossdhu's ancestral treasures were lost but were replaced over the years by new and special Highland artifacts that are spectacular.

COLQUHOUN history is as amazing in the twentieth century as when the old castle, Rossdhu, was built on the same plot in the thirteenth century. There have been grotesque scenes of Black Magic, deathly-dangerous love, and the clash of arms here. Thus it is more than a eminent country house with the nearby ruins of the historic castle in one of the best-known and most beautiful settings known to man. Above all, it is the home of COLQUHOUNS/CALHOUNS worldwide.

Though construction began on the modern
mansion in 1772, it wasn't completed until
1773. SIR JAMES 23RD consulted many
prominent architects of the day including
Robert Adam. It has been suggested that
this famous architect was the designer.
There is evidence that Sir James
considered Sir James Clerk of Penicuik,
and John Baxter to build the new home,
but by this time Adam and Baxter were
working together. The Baxter son has been
established as the designer in his own
right with evidence that his hallmark is
at the back of the house.

Visitors enter into the main hall and
immediately their attention is drawn to
the elegant cantilever staircase with
wrought iron banisters. Many of the
castles were built with a one-room main
hall to deter their enemies in the event
of an attack. This staircase leads to the
first and second floors. Hanging nearby is
the head of a reindeer. It was found in
1935 by scouts in Port O'Rossdhu and has
been identified as from the second ice age
and is some 10,000 years old. On the
staircase a view of the cupola can be
seen.

The choice decor on the second floor is
the hand-painted silk wall covering
designed especially for the room in Hong
Kong by Chinese craftsmen. The measurement
and fittings were carried out by the
estate joiner whose family has served the
COLQUHOUNS for many years. Curtains and
window seat covers were made in Hong Kong

at the same time. A pair of gilt Adam
mirrors surmounted by floral carving and a
stag's head, the family crest, hang on the
walls. Over one of the doors is a carving
of the same design. This was one of the
treasures sold in earlier days and was
listed in a catalog for the sale of
antiques. Sir Ivar, recognizing it as
part of the collection which belonged to
Rossdhu, purchased it. Proudly it hangs
in the same spot today .

Two settees and seven shield back chairs
in pink and gold floral silk were probably
made to a design by George Hepplewhite,
and the impressive mahogany breakfront
bookcase is of the Chippendale period. An
unusual Spanish chest with many richly
carved and inlaid drawers sits beside the
fireplace.

The grand drawing room, added in the 19th
century, now forms a family portrait
gallery. These pictures were placed by
SIR IAIN COLQUHOUN, carefully labelled and
identified. Unfortunately some of them
still show signs of the damage suffered in
the fire which swept through the room
early in this century. Sir Iain was
serving in Egypt with his regiment at the
time and received a cable from the estate
factor telling him of the fire.

His one word reply: "Rebuild".

Many family favorites were collected and
brought into the drawing room. Probably
one of the most interesting and the most

battered by age and use, is the workbox
which was once the property of MARY, QUEEN
OF SCOTS. Perhaps she left it behind as a
momento of one of her visits to Rossdhu
Castle.

SIR IAIN used a small room adjacent to the
drawing room to showcase his collection of
china and pictures of famous
prizefighters. He was Lightweight Boxing
Champion of the British Army, founder and
chairman of the National Trust for
Scotland.

The ceiling in the library is the finest
in the house, and rumor has it that it was
in the drawing room in the original 18th
century home. Two walls comprise the
resting place of impressive mahogany
bookcases, no doubt made for the room when
it became the library. Books with calf-
bound backs, many with the book-plates of
SIR JAMES COLQUHOUN, builder of the home,
fill the shelves. Religious pictures were
hung on the walls. Nine mahogany camel
back chairs with seats were upholstered by
LADY COLQUHOUN herself from designs in
the Victoria and Albert Museum. LADY
COLQUHOUN'S bedroom is dominated by an
impressive Italian four-poster bed
upholstered in pink damask. The present
LADY COLQUHOUN still occupies this room.

The dining room balances the large drawing
room wing and was probably added to the
home at the same time. Portraits of the
family in later days decorate the walls.
Some of the treasured ones were purchased

and put back in their place when they had sufficient funds. No doubt many irreplaceable treasures have been lost.

Most of the furniture in the dining room is of the late Georgian period and probably was bought for the room when it was first built. The centerpiece attraction is the French ormolu and crystal chandelier. Large green glass bottles on the mantle were used on H. M. ships to store castor oil for the ship's crew.

The Scottish word "policies" is defined in the Oxford Dictionary as the enclosed, planted and partly embellished park or demesne land lying around a country seat or gentleman's residence. This is a veritable habitat for wild life of varying descriptions. Most of the birds and animals spend the winters on the islands in the Loch and fly or swim to the mainland when summer visitors arrive on the islands.

A fascinating game room holds stuffed birds and mammals gathered from his policies during the middle of the 19th century by JOHN COLQUHOUN, great grandfather of the present Chief. At first this collection was to have been his own, but as an enticement to his sons he allowed their genus to be added.

The prime importance to him was not to shoot just a quantity of each species but to make them as interesting as possible.

For the sake of contrast he put up the most common of owls in one case and of three house sparrows cased together; one is normal and the other mutants. The albino corn-bunting, shot by his eldest son in 1857, sits beside the ordinary one.

Some of the specimens have disintegrated with time, such as the woodpeckers, snakes, and lizards. Still available for the visitor's eyes are the old black Scotch rat, the waxwings he shot in his garden and the dog badger trapped by his two younger sons.

Although John enjoyed the sport of hunting for his collection, he was no wanton killer of wildlife. This was quite acceptable by the standards of the day, but he was remorseful to his dying day and was bitterly ashamed of shooting a female osprey nesting on the top of a ruin on Inchgalbraith, thus bringing to an end the nesting of ospreys on Loch Lomondside.

His life spent as a sportsman was documented in "The Moor and the Loch" and other books which he wrote on wildlife and fishing of the area, most of it around his beloved Rossdhu. As a lad he shot the first rabbit on the grounds of Luss, and in 1822 the now very rare kite was still around on Loch Lomondside as it nested in an oak tree on Rossdhu lawn.

Birds found according to Major Henry Douglas-Home on Rossdhu and in the vicinity were Red Crested Pochard, Great

Northern Diver, Long-Tailed Duck, Osprey,
Red-Tailed Kite, Golden Eagle, White-
tailed Eagle, Dotterel, Bar-tailed Godwit,
Whimbrel, Turtle Dove, Stock Dove,
Wryneck, Great Grey Shrike, Waxwing, Jay,
Fulmar, Capercaillie, and Killdeer Plover.

This eight or more miles of brilliant land
mass called Rossdhu is truly a sight to
behold.

** A good portion of this chapter was
taken from a booklet written by Sir Ivar
COLQUHOUN Br. It was printed and Produced
in Great Britain by Photo Precision Ltd.,
St. Ives, Hunts.

MUSIC OF THE HIGHLANDS

* * *

"The Highlanders delight much in musicke, but chiefly in harps and clairschoes of their own fashion. The strings of the clairschoes are made of brass wire, and the strings of the harps of sinews; which strings they strike with their nayles growing long, or else with an instrument appointed for that use." (From: "Vide" Anno Domini 1597.)

The harp was played as a primary instrument until the mid sixteenth century. How the bagpipes with their noisy and unharmonious sounds banished the soft and expressive harp is unknown. (From: Campbell's Journey through North Britain. 1808).

From: Footnotes from "Lady of the Lake": Though some do consider the bagpipes noisy their sound has thrilled Scot's hearts over the ages, inspired the soldier in battle and struck fear into the enemy. It has also welcomed visitors, lamented the dead, and soothed the breast of the troubled. It was in Scotland that music of the pipes was created to play a classical form that they call the Piobaireachd. It has come down through the years as unwritten melody, free flowing and subject to the personal interpretation of each performer. This Piobaireachd (pronounced "pea-broch with the ch as in 'loch'") is played in competitions and is considered the original form of pipe music played on the highland bagpipe."

Nevertheless it is now and has been since the sixteenth century, the musical instrument played on all Scottish occasions with the fifes and drums. However, during a period of time bagpipes were banned by the Reformers in the Lowlands as being sinful and then by the Whigs. After battle at Culloden in 1745, the bagpipes became the national instrument of Scotland again.

The Highland chieftains until a late period retained in their service the bard as a family officer. Legend has it that the bard was skilled in the genealogy of all the Highland families setting to music his own lyrics, sometimes annoying and obnoxious to the listeners but telling vivid accounts of their battles in the glens and mountains.

"The connoisseurs in pipe-music affect to discover in a well-composed pibroch, the imitative sounds of march, conflict, pursuit, and all the current of a heady fight. To this opinion Dr. Beattie has given his suffrage, in the following elegant passage; 'A pibroch is a species of tune, peculiar, I think, to the Highlands and Western Isles of Scotland. It is performed on the bagpipe, and differs totally from

all other music. Its rhythm is so
irregular, and its notes, especially in
the quick movement, so mixed and
huddled together that a stranger finds
it impossible to reconcile his ear to
it, so as to perceive its modulation.
Some of these pibrochs, being intended
to represent a battle, begin with a
grave motion resembling a march: then
gradually quicken into the onset; run
off with noisy confusion, and turbulent
rapidity, to imitate the conflict and
pursuit; then swell into a few
flourishes of triumphant joy: and
perhaps close with the wild and low
wailings of a funeral procession.'"
(From Essays on Laughter and Ludicrous
Composition, chap.iii.)

Through the generations musicians have
improved their pibrochs and delighted
audiences with song. The most
significant song from Scotland was
derived from Sir Walter Scott's "Lady
of the Lake" and is the glorious "Hail
to the Chief" played on many occasions
as the President of the United States
appears. Perhaps the most famous of all
the Scottish tunes is "Auld Lang Syne"
sung by school children, New Year's eve
revelers, and friends singing sad
goodbyes to friends.

Scott had the unique privilege of his
poetic offerings in "Lady of the Lake"
being arranged into a songs by Schubert
(1797-1826). His songs remained the
best known adaptations of Scott. "The

Lady of the Lake" provided the foundation for the first opera based on Scott's works. Who other than Shakespeare, was the British writer capable of composing the most operas?

Besides the bard as a family officer each chief had a piper whose position was most important as demonstrated by his being held in high esteem. He was overseer of certain property for his support and ranked above the other members of the chief's retinue until the passing of the Heritable Jurisdiction Act of 1747 which deprived them of the land.

The piper's "gillie" was his young boy servant to carry his pipes when not being played. Within a generation most of the old pipers had disappeared, many of them crossing over to America. Only after a competition in 1781 when the Highland Society of London conducted auditions in Scotland did the bagpipe come back into its own.

*** A good portion of this chapter was taken from the footnotes in "The Lady of the Lake" 1830 version written by Sir Walter Scott.

SCOTTISH GAMES

Games of Scotland excite descendents of the various Clans today as festivals are held in many states in America as well as lands all over the world where Scotsmen live. Scot athletes were chosen as teenagers to learn who were the strongest and most agile and who were capable of making a spectacular team with their sheer brawn in front of viewers.

The parade of the Tartans is a distinctive sight to see as Clan members march across the stage to the stirring music of the pipes, fifes and drums. Notable of all of the dances, the Highland Fling and the Sword Dance are the favorites of visitors. When the Queen's Highlanders and the Coldstream Guards perform, it's truly a presentation to behold. (See dance descriptions below)

An 18 hole kilted golf tournament, Highland and country dance competition, pipe and drum band competition, New England harp championships, open air worship services, 5K run, battle axe, rugby tournament, international polo matches, sheep herding, Kirking of the Tartans, workshops, Ceilidh, whiskey tasting, address to the Haggis, and Scottish vendors with their wares, foods, and video tapes of Scotland and members of some of the Clans all create an exciting week-ends for visitors in many areas of the country.

The ancient and honorable sport of Haggis
Hurling grew from the very humble origins
from many years ago where a small village
of Aughnaclory stood by the Falls of
Dromach, on the River Dromach, Sutherland,
Scotland. Each day, the men would tend
their sheep, and the women would go up
from the village and "Hurl the Haggis"
luncheons across the river to their
menfolk. A hurling Haggis weighing one
and a half pounds is the amount of food
necessary to feed a Highlander for a day.

The Caber toss, probably the most famous
of all the heavy events, dates back to the
16th century, where there are references
to "ye casting of the bar". This event is
also one of the most misunderstood.
Distance has no bearing on the outcome of
the event. The object of the contest is
to toss the caber end-over-end so the
small end falls directly away from the
contestant. Each competitor has three
attempts to toss the caber. All tosses are
scored. Because the caber and the terrain
at each game are slightly different, there
can be no uniform records. Cabers average
19 feet in length and 120 pounds in
weight.

The Hammer Throw which was begun as an
informal contest between two young men in
front of a blacksmith shop in the
Highlands of Scotland has grown into an
internationally recognized Olympic event.
Today's hammer is twenty-two pounds in
weight and the competitor is judged on the
best of three throws.

113

Weigh Toss and Weight Throw both comprise a three-part competition using two metal weights,one twenty-eight pounds and the other fifty-six pounds. Both weights are thrown for distance and the fifty-six pound weight is also tossed for height. In each event the competitors are given three tries each and scored on the best of three.

The Sheaf Toss event obviously began in the agricultural regions of Scotland. A sixteen pound sheaf of hay enclosed in a burlap bag is tossed with a three-tined pitchfork over a bar. The sheaf must clear the bar without touching. Each competitor is given three opportunities at each height, after which the bar is raised six inches and the competition repeats until all competitors but one are eliminated.

The Stone Of Strength is known in Gaelic as Clachneart and is similar to the Olympic shot put. The stone is twenty-seven pounds and is made of heavy granite. Each competitor is allowed three throws and is judged on the longest throw only.

Clan tents are displayed over a wide field, each with its flag and colors flying in the wind. Some members of each Clan are present during the days of the games to educate and inform the visitors about their heritage. Often times many COLQUHOUN/CALHOUNS find their lineage back

to the UMFRIDUS DE COLQUHOUN AND
KILPATRICK in 1190 AD.

On the entertainment stage noted Scots
sing, play their instruments and dance to
the delight of the audience as they sit to
listen or walk around the grounds to visit
the tents. Pipes are the music of choice
of the Scots. To create a band, a Pipe
Major and a Lead Drummer are essential
people of the band though the Pipe Major
may not play a note. He is responsible
for the organization of the band and the
selection of the music and its order in
the program.

The dancing competition began as an
athletic event. The Sword dance (Gillie
Callum) is believed to be the oldest of
Scottish dances. Sword and scabbard were
placed on the ground in the form of a
cross, and if the dancer's feet managed to
avoid touching either one, it was
understood that the clan would be blessed
with good fortune in the coming battle.
However, if the sword or scabbard were
disturbed, the prediction was defeat.

The Highland Fling, another of the oldest
traditional dances of Scotland, is
believed to be the dance of victory in
battle. The dancer performed with a
Scottish shield called a Targe. Since the
ancient Targe contained a sharp steel
spike extending out of the center, the
dancer had to be very careful in the
execution of his steps.

Seann Triubhas was the dance intended to express the Scotman's displeasure for an old law which at one time forbade the wearing of kilts. In Gaelic, Seann Triubhas (pronounced Shawn Trues) means "old trouser". The name is a derisive reference to the law enforced after the unsuccessful Rebellion of 1745 in support of "Bonnie Price Charlie" when kilts, bagpipes and other Highland traditional trappings were forbidden. Many of the steps of the dance are intended to indicate the Scotman's efforts to kick off the trousers, and the quick steps at the end of the dance suggest the freedom of movement afforded by the kilt.

Ceilidh, a Gaelic word (pronounced kay-lee) is the family fun time where entertainment is at its peak. This unstructured party event brings wee ones and older folk together in a evening of singing, dancing, clapping, story-telling and jokes to make a lifetime of memories for Scots when they get together. In days of yore in Scotland the party was spontaneous when ancestors gathered in a home, a kirk hall, pub or inn. It was not a professional time and no two ever were alike.

Kirking of the Tartans is the worship service held at the end of a series of the Scottish games. After the invocation scriptures from the Old Testament and from the New were read. Blessing of the Tartans ended the week-end event with memorial roll call and the laying of the wreath "Flowers of the Forest" and the benediction.

Tartans are basic for the Scottish Highland Dress. Originally many, many years ago they were worn for warmth. When in the woods at night either in battle array or moving from one place to the other, the Highlander would wet his Tartan until soaked. Then, he wrapped it around him and laid down on the ground to sleep. They declared this kept them warm.

Complete outfits can be purchased from specialty shops in the price range of $900 and up. For an average size man eight yards of 100% pure new wool worsted in light or full weight cloth will make a made-to-measure kilt. Barathea dress argyll or border tweed argyll jacket, leather sporran with a set of straps and chains, sword kilt pin, kilt hose and a pair of black leather Ghillie brogues complete the formal dresswear. Clothing worn in Scotland for the winter months can be made of the pure new wool worsted, but, when worn in warmer weather whether at home or abroad, lighter fabrics are more appropriate, more comfortable, and quite acceptable.

According to tradition, Scottish Highland Games were originated by the kings and chiefs of Scotland as a means of selecting the best men available by testing them for strength, stamina, accuracy and agility on the battle field.

Today some come to the games not knowing that their origin was in Scotland and leave with a determination to trace their lineages as far back as possible. They take great pride and pleasure in perpetuating the culture of Scotland.

COLQUHOUN/CALHOUN

FACTS AND HYPERBOLE FROM SCOTLAND
****

A Highland Chief, being as absolute in his patriarchal authority as any prince, had a corresponding number of officers attached to his person. His body guards were chosen from his Clan for strength, activity, and fond loyalty to his person.

These domestic officers who were independent of the "Gardes de corps" made up the establishment of a Highland Chief:
1) the henchman, his personal servant;
2) the bard, the musician for the Clan;
3) the bladier, his spokesman;
4) (Gillie being boy servant) Gillie more, the sword bearer;
5) the Gillie-casflue, who carried the Chief, if on foot, over the fords;
6) Gillie-constraine, who leads the Chief's horse;
7) Gillie, Trushanarinsh, the baggageman;
8) the piper;
9) the piper's gillie or attendant who carries all of the bagpipes and equipment:
(From Letters from Scotland, vol ii p. 15)

An old Scot's legend narrated the merry doings of the good old times when he was a follower of Rob Roy MacGregor. This leader, on one occasion, thought it proper to make a raid upon the lower part of the Loch Lomond district, and summoned all the heritors and farmers to meet at the Kirk of Drymen, to pay him black-mail (a tribute for forbearance and protection).

As this invitation was supported by a band
of thirty or forty stout fellows, only one
gentleman, an ancestor of Mr. Grahame of
Gartmore, ventured to decline compliance.
Rob Roy instantly swept his land of all he
could drive away, and among the spoils was
a bull of the old Scottish wild breed,
whose ferocity occasionally had plagued
them all.

The Hero's Targe is a rock so named in the
Forest of Glenfinlas by which a tumultuous
cataract takes its course. This wild
place is said in former times to have
afforded refuge to an outlaw, who was
supplied with provisions by a woman, who
lowered them down from the brink of the
precipice above. His water he procured
for himself by letting down a flagon tied
to a string, into the black pool beneath
the fall. (SIR WALTER SCOTT)

Each young Chief, to prove his worthiness
as a warrior, was required to lead his
Clan on a successful raid against a
neighboring sept, the Saxons or the
Lowlanders. An apology was always
forthcoming to the neighbors and the
Saxons but not the Lowlanders. The Gael
historians had always remembered that the
Lowlands had belonged at some remote past
period to their Celtic forefathers. This
was vindication for all of the ravages
they could make on the unfortunate
districts which lay within their reach.

Sir James Grant, husband of ANNE COLQUHOUN
through her inheritance, was 6th Baronet

of Luss. He retained for posterity a
letter of apology from Cameron of Lochiel
whose men had plundered a farm called
Moines which was occupied by one of the
Grants. Grant was assured that it was an
error. The party should have caused the
foray on the province of Moray (a Lowland
district), where as he cooly observed,
"all men take their prey." SIR WALTER
SCOTT)

The Gaels were not all bad as the
following legendary incident illustrates.
Early in the fifteenth century, John Gunn,
a noted Cateran (Highland robber), often
raided Invernesshire and levied blackmail
up to the walls of the provincial capitol.
A garrison was then maintained in the
castle of that town and their pay was
usually transmitted in specie, under the
guard of a small escort.

It happened that the officer who commanded
this party was ordered to halt at a
miserable country inn. About nightfall a
stranger in Highland dress and of very
handsome appearance entered the same
house. Separate accommodations being
impossible, Gunn offered the newly-arrived
guest a part of his supper, which was
accepted with reluctance. By their
conversation with this new acquaintance he
determined that the Highlander knew well
all the passes of the country. Gunn asked
him eagerly to accompany him on the next
morning's journey as guide. The
Highlander hesitated for a moment, and
then consented to be his escort.

The next morning while traveling through a solitary and dreary glen, the conversation turned to John Gunn. "Would you like to see him?' asked the guide. Without waiting for an answer, he whistled and Gunn was surrounded by an assembly of well armed Highlanders. His escape was impossible.

"Stranger," resume the guide, "I am that very John Gunn by whom you feared to be intercepted. I came to the inn last night with the express purpose of learning your route, that I and my followers might ease you of your charge by the road. But I am incapable of betraying the trust you put in me, and having convinced you that you were in my power, I can only dismiss you unplundered and uninjured."

He then gave Gunn directions for his journey and disappeared with his party as quickly as they had presented themselves. (SIR WALTER SCOTT).

On his deathbed Rob Roy learned that one of his enemies intended to visit him. The invalid Rob Roy said, "Raise me from my bed and throw my plaid around me. Bring my claymore, dirk, and pistols. It shall never be said that a foe saw Rob Roy MacGregor defenceless and unarmed."

His visitor, who was reported to be a MacLarens, entered and paid his compliments, inquiring after the good health of his formidable neighbor. Rob

Roy kept a cool, haughty civility during
their short encounter and as soon as this
visitor left the house, he said, "All is
over. Let the piper play 'Ha til mi
tulidh (we return no more).'" He died
before the dirge was finished.
(Introduction to Rob Roy, Waverly Novels,
vol vii p. 85.)

**** ALL OF THE ABOVE TAKEN FROM FOOTNOTES
OF "THE LADY OF THE LAKE" BY SIR WALTER
SCOTT. PUBLISHED IN 1830.

COLQUHOUN/CALHOUN

SCOTTISH TABLE FARE

xxxxx
Never start a meal without a Scottish
Blessing

Oh Lord,wha blessed the loaves and fishes.
Look doon upon these twa bit dishes.
And tho' the taffies be but sma',
Lord, mak'them plenty for us a'.
But if our stomachs they do fill,
'Twill be another miracle.

ANON

If that one is not acceptable, try this:

Some hae meat that canna eat,
An'some wad eat that want it;
But we hae meat, an' we can eat,
Sae let the Lord be thankit!!
AN OLD COVENANTER'S GRACE

ARBROATH FISH SOUP

1 Cod's head or 2-3 haddocks heads
2 onions
1 small carrot
a slice turnip
1 stick celery
4 ounces flour
A pot-posy:
2 sprigs parsley,
1 bay leaf,
1 blade mace.
Salt and pepper
1 ounce butter
1 pint milk
1 quart water

COLQUHOUN/CALHOUN

1 small slice of fish (opt.)

Wash the head and put it on with cold
water and a little salt. Bring slowly to
a boil and remove the scum. Add the
prepared vegetables and the pot posy.
Simmer 1 1/2 hours or longer, and strain.
Season. Remove skin and bone from the
slice of fish, chop small, add to the
stock and cook for five minutes.

PARTAN BREE
(This rich cream of crab soup originated
with fishermen in the western Scottish
islands. Partan is Gaelic for Crab and
Bree means Broth.)

1 cup chicken broth
1/4 cup long-grain rice
1 tablespoon butter
1 cup baked, cleaned fresh crabmeat
1 flat anchovy fillet, minced or 1 tsp.
anchovy paste
2 cups hot milk
1/2 cup heavy cream
Freshly ground white pepper to taste
1 tablespoon. chopped fresh watercress.

Combine chicken broth, rice and butter in
a large saucepan. Bring to a boil; reduce
heat. Cook slowly, covered, about 20
minutes until rice is done. Add 1/2 cup
crabmeat and anchovy or paste. Puree in
blender. Return to rinsed saucepan;
reheat over low heat. Add hot milk, cream
and remaining 1/2 cup crabmeat. Season
with pepper. Cook slowly 1 or 2 minutes.

125

Serve garnished with watercress. (serves 4)

SALMON SOUP

Trimmings of a fresh salmon
Bones of 1 or 2 fresh whiting
1 tablespoon chopped parsley
Handful of brown bread crumbs
Potato flour or mashed potato
1 small carrot
1 slice turnip
1 stick celery
1 small onion
Water
Small slice fresh salmon

Put into fish kettle the head, bones, fins and skins of the salmon, along with the bones of the whiting (these make all the difference) and the prepared vegetables. Cover amply with cold water, bringing to a boil, add salt, and boil gently for at least an hour. Strain, and remove all fat and oil. Thicken with potato flour or mashed potato. Add some scallops of uncooked salmon, the chopped parsley and the brown bread crumbs. As soon as the salmon is cooked, the soup is ready.

CAULIFLOWER SLAW
(Serve with poultry or game)

1 medium head (about 1 1/2 lbs. cauliflower
2 large carrots scraped

COLQUHOUN/CALHOUN

1/2 cup chopped green onions and tops
1/2 cup chopped fresh parsley
1/3 cup vegetable oil
3 tablespoons cider vinegar
1/4 teaspoon dry mustard
1/4/teaspoon curry powder
Salt and pepper to taste.

Wash cauliflower, remove and discard
outside leaves. Break into small
flowerets and slice each one thinly.
Quarter carrots and slice thinly. Combine
cauliflower and carrots with green onions
and parsley in a large bowl. Combine
remaining ingredients and pour over
vegetables. Refrigerate, cover at least
an hour before serving.

CULLEN SKINK

1 large smoked finnon haddock- 2 lbs.
1 medium sliced onion
1 1/2 pints milk (3 cups)
2 tablespoons butter
8 ounces cooked mashed potato (2 cups)
Salt and pepper

Place haddock in shallow pan, skin side
down with just enough cold water to cover
it, bring to boil, then simmer for 4
minutes. Turn the fish and take off skin,
and add the sliced onion, cover, simmer
very gently for 10 minutes. Take fish
out, and remove all bones, then put them
back in the stock and simmer again for 20
minutes then strain. Put the milk and the
stock in saucepan, add the fish, bring to

boiling point then add enough mashed
potato to make it creamy and the
consistency you like. Add the butter in
very small pieces and season to taste.
The last of the butter added should hardly
melt, but run in little yellow rivulets
through the soup-stew.

KEDGEREE
1 pound cold smoked haddock
1/4 pound rice
2 hard boiled eggs
2 ounces butter
Salt and Pepper
Cayenne pepper

Boil and dry the rice. Divide the fish
into small flakes. Cut the egg whites
into small slices and sieve the yolks.
Melt butter in saucepan, add it to the
fish, rice, egg whites, salt, pepper and
cayenne and stir until hot.

Turn mixture onto a hot serving dish.
Press into the shape of a pyramid with a
fork, decorate with sieved egg yolks and
serve immediately.

ECCLES CAKES

Flake or rough puff pastry using 6 oz.
flour.
1/2 ounces butter
1/4 ounces sugar
2 ounces currants

3/4 ounces chopped peel
1/4 teaspoon mixed spice
Small amount of grated nutmeg.

Roll out pastry 1/4 inch thick, cut into four inch rounds. Cream fat and sugar, add currants, peel and spice and place a good teaspoon of the mixture in the center of each round of pastry. Gather the edges together, pinch firmly and form into a flat cake; reverse the cake and roll gently till the fruit begins to show through. Make two cuts on top of each, brush with water and dust with castor sugar. Bake in a hot oven (425 F.) Makes 12-14 cakes. Cooking time 20 minutes.

SPORRAN SPICY RAISIN BISCUITS

4 oz. self-raising flour
1/2 teaspoon ground cinnamon
4 ounces castor sugar
4 ounces butter
1 tablespoon milk
2 beaten eggs
3 ounces seedless raisins

Sift flour and cinnamon into a basin. Rub in butter. Stir in sugar, eggs, milk and raisins. Mix to a stiff dough. Knead lightly on a well-floured board. Roll out thinly. Put into round pan 2- 2 1/2 inches across. Place a little spray on a buttered baking-sheet. Bake towards the top of a moderately hot oven, 375 degrees until crisp and golden.
10-15 minutes.

TANTALLON CAKES

(This lemon-flavored cookie is named for Tantallon Castle, a rose-colored ruined stronghold a few miles east of North Berwick, now a national monument.)

1/2 cup (1 stick of butter, softened)
1/3 cup sugar, preferably superfine
1 teaspoon grated lemon rind
1 large egg beaten
2 tablespoons cornstarch
1/8/ teaspoon salt
About 1 1/4 cups all purpose flour
Confectioners' sugar.

Cream butter with a flat wooden spoon in a large deep bowl. Add sugar gradually, beating until light and fluffy. Stir in lemon rind. Add egg; mix well. Gradually sift in cornstarch, salt and flour, 1/2 cup at a time, using enough flour until mixture can be pressed together to form a ball. Turn out dough on a lightly floured smooth, cool surface. Gently roll out with a wooden rolling pin to 1/4 inch thickness. keeping the shape as circular as possible. With a floured cutter cut into 2 1/2 inch circles. Prick tops of each circle all over with a fork. With a spatula, remove to an ungreased baking sheet, placing 1/2 inches apart. Bake in a preheated 325 degree oven 12/15 minutes or until pale golden and firm to the touch. With a spatula, remove at once to a wire rack to cool completely. Sprinkle with confectioners' sugar.

This makes about 16 cookies.

NEVER FAIL SHORTBREAD

2 cups all-purpose flour
3/4 cup rice flour
pinch of salt
8 ounces unsalted butter
3/4 cup superfine sugar (put granulated sugar in a blender until it's dust.

Mix flour and salt in a bowl,
Cut butter into small pieces and add to flour, working both together with fingertips until well blended.
Add sugar and knead on a floured board until smooth.
Oil the mold, cookie cutters, etc.
Dust with flour and shake off the excess.
Bake at 325 degrees for 35-45 minutes until pale brown.
Cool on baking sheet and serve with fruit and/or whipped cream.

Another shortbread recipe that has proven to be satisfactory.

SHORTBREAD

2 cups all-purpose flour,
1/2 cup sugar
1 heaping tablespoon cornstarch,
1/2 butter, softened

Place all of the dry ingredients in a mixing bowl and blend well. Put in butter using a heavy-duty electric mixer or pastry blender. Knead the dough by hand for just a moment and form it into a circle 3/4 " thick on a non-stick baking sheet, and flute the edges. Prick the whole circle with a fork into pie-piece shapes. Bake in a preheated 325 degree oven for 1/2 hour, or until it just begins to turn a light golden brown. Allow it to cool for a few minutes, and then remove it to a rack for the final cooling. This recipe works best if the bread is too thick instead of too thin.

BLACK CURRANT JAM

4 pounds black currants
3 pints water
6 pounds sugar

Clean fruit and remove all stems. Place black currants in a preserving pan with the water and simmer until fruit is tender and contents of pan greatly reduced, stirring occasionally to prevent sticking. Add the sugar, stir until dissolved then boil rapidly until setting point is reached. Pot and cover in the usual way.

RASP JAM

4 pounds hulled raspberries
4 pounds sugar

COLQUHOUN/CALHOUN

Wash fruit and simmer very gently in its
own juice 15-30 minutes. Add sugar, stir
till dissolved, then boil rapidly until
setting point is reached. Pot and cover
in the usual way.

SHEPHERD'S PIE

1 pound cold beef or mutton
1 onion
1/2 pint gravy
2 pounds cooked mashed potatoes
Egg or milk
Salt and pepper to taste.

Remove any skin, bone or gristle and cut
the meat into small dice, parboil and
finely chop the onion and place in a pie
dish with the meat and gravy. Season to
taste. Cover with mashed potatoes and
decorate top to look like a pie crust.
Glaze with beaten egg or milk. Bake in
moderate oven 350 degrees Fahrenheit until
thoroughly heated and surface is well
browned.

HAGGIS

1 beef heart cut into 2" wide strips
1 1/2 finely chopped yellow onion
1 pound beef liver
4 tablespoons Scotch
1/2 pound lamb stew meat cut in 1" pieces
2 cups toasted Oatmeal for 375 Degrees ten
minutes.

SEASONINGS
2 teaspoons salt,
1/2 teaspoon pepper,
1 teaspoon thyme
1/2 teaspoon rosemary
1/4 teaspoon freshly ground nutmeg

CASING
Beef caps (or any kind of sausage casing)
1 cup distilled white vinegar
1/2 tablespoon salt

Place the beef heart in a 4 quart covered
pot and barely cover with cold water.
Simmer, covered, for 1 hour and 10
minutes. Add the beef liver and lamb stew
meat, and cover and simmer for 20 minutes.
Remove the contents of the pot and cool.
Reserve 1 cup of the liquid. Grind
everything coarsely (almost to hamburger
consistency). In a large bowl mix all the
ingredients, except for the beef caps,
vinegar, and salt for soaking. Mix well
and set aside. Rinse the beef caps in
cold water. Turn them inside out and soak
them in 2 quarts cold water with the salt
and vinegar for 1/2 hour. Drain them and
rinse very well, inside and out. Fill
casings with the meat mixture and tie off
the ends. Prick the haggis all over with
a sharp fork. Will expand the filling
(remember that when filling the casings).
Place in steamer and steam for 1 hour and
20 minutes. It can be served with beef or
lamb gravy.

This dish tastes slightly like liver but
has been the staple

of The Scottish diet.

MICROWAVE HAGGIS

(This recipe is similar to the one above but eliminates the casing.)
1 pound calves liver
1 pound mild sausage
1 pound ground lamb
1 1/2 cups steel cut oats
1 cup chopped onion
1 teaspoon coriander
1 teaspoon black pepper
1 teaspoon red pepper
1 teaspoon nutmeg
2 teaspoon salt
1 cup undiluted beef bouillon

Cook the liver halfway and grind fine in a meat grinder or food processor. Cook the sausage and lamb halfway, drain grease and break up into small bits. Mix all ingredients very well in a large microwave cooking dish. Micro on high for thirty minutes stirring every ten minutes to prevent crust from forming. This is very spicy and hot. Peppers may be reduced to taste.

Serve with crackers for appetizer and with turnips and potatoes for a main dish.

CHICKEN STOVIES

3 pounds chicken cut in pieces
3 onions

2 ounces butter
1 pint stock
2 1/2 pounds potatoes
2 tablespoons chopped parsley
Salt to taste.

Brown chicken pieces in half the butter.
Remove from the pan and fill with
alternate layers of sliced potato, sliced
onion and chicken, seasoning as you go,
and dotting with butter. Top with a layer
of potatoes and pour in the giblet stock.
Replace lid tightly and simmer for 2 1/2
hours, checking occasionally to prevent
drying. Sprinkle with parsley before
serving.

A SCOTS VENISON

For a great hunting party a circle of
sportsmen, gradually surrounded a great
space and successively narrowed it,
brought immense quantities of deer
together for the kill. The dressed
venison was compressed between two slats
of wood to force out the blood and render
it extremely hard. Then they ate it raw
convincing their French guests that it was
a great delicacy.

These recipes are but a few of the
favorites for the Scot's table to be
served with kippers, long kail and
pottage, bannocks of barley meal, good
salt herring, a cup of good ale, onions,
radishes, pease boiled and raw, abundance
of mouthfuls of skate, sheep's head broth,
fresh ox feet, crabs, winkles, speldies

(dried fish), haddocks, and broth with barley and brandy. After the meal a touch of snuff ended the satisfying day with dancing and drinking.
* * * * *

Most of these recipes were taken from the Scottish Banner and are authentic Scot's fare.

COLQUHOUN/CALHOUN

THE SCOT-IRISH
IN ULSTER

Use of the term Scotch-Irish is incorrect.
Scotch is the well-known alcoholic drink,
the Scottish liquor made in Scotland and
famous the world over. The term should
never be used as a Scot, or Scottish
gentleman. Scot-Irish though not wrong
could be said better as Ulster-Scot. This
was a term developed on the American
frontier to separate those who had passed
through the Emerald Isle on their way to
America.

Their interlude in America may have been
for a period long enough for their ship to
take on cargo and passengers, for a
generation or two, or perhaps as long as
hundreds of years. These people were
frequently but not always, the rebels from
Scotland. From the time of Cromwell
through the clearances in Scotland of the
18th century, the English as a means of
getting rid of the unwanted had been
planting them in Ulster, the West Indies,
America, and Australia.

CLAN COLQUHOUN members shortened the
spelling of their name to COLHOUN while in
Ulster where many of them live today. The
common spelling of our name in the U. S.
and Canada was changed to CALHOUN. No
matter the spelling, the origins are the
same with the lineage going back to CLAN
COLQUHOUN on the western shores of Loch
Lomond in Scotland. There are many in the
world outside of Scotland today who still

use the old name, COLQUHOUN, particularly
on the west coast of United States.

Some historians do not agree that all of
the Scots who relocated into Ulster were
rebels or undesirables. One Virginian, D.
Bell, stated "The English Crown, anxious
to permanently establish its presence in
Ulster, began offering grants of land to
those in Great Britain who would relocate.
The colonial governor of Virginia urged
this same group of people to settle in the
Shenandoah Valley to serve as a buffer
against the Indians. These are the hardy
people who did not shrink from a battle!"

He also said,"Besides the offer of land,
their Presbyterian religion was allowed to
be more freely practiced in Ulster than in
Great Britain or Scotland where
Catholicism was the choice of the Crown.
After a while when escalating rents and
free practice of their religious beliefs
in Ulster did not meet their expectations,
a move to America and other lands seemed
more promising."

In addition British trade policies
discriminated against Ireland, making it
necessary for the Scottish Christians in
Ulster to migrate to a more suitable
environment. Failure of the potato crops
for several successive years in the 1800s
created a devastating famine for Ireland's
people. Approximately two million of them
were lost either through death or
emigration to another land by the middle
of the nineteenth century.

COLQUHOUN/CALHOUN

"The first wave of migration lasted from 1700 to 1740, with most initially coming to those colonies where religious liberty was the greatest. Pennsylvania was one choice. The second wave, including a group of the Highland Scots, began about 1745-1750, following Bonnie Prince Charles' defeat and the first of several famines in Ireland. Movement of these people also were to Lanark, Canada and to the Barbados Islands.

They were always Scots first and Ulstermen second, but never Irish. The name Scot-Irish was used in America by these people to separate themselves from the Irish, who settled neighborhood districts in the coastal cities and really loyal Scot businessmen. These so called Scot-Irish were often enticed by agents located in most of the cities of Ulster, who offered a better life to all who leave for America. Land speculators leased or sold them farm land. Some came as indentured servants.

Many settled in North and South Carolina, but most decided to live in Pennsylvania and Virginia. However, they can be found from Maine's Waldo and Hancock Counties in the north, to Georgia's Columbia and Richmond Counties in the south. Their influence can be felt in the names of our cities and counties. Surely Ulster County, New York and COLQUHOUN District in GA were not named by a Scot-Irishman from the old countries.

COLQUHOUN/CALHOUN

One William COLQUHOUN, as a planter in
Antigua, made bond for 1000 pounds to
Alexander McAlister, planter in Dominica
on the one hand and Robert Graham, planter
in Antigua, on the other, dated March 4,
1778. (From: "Scottish Settlers in North
America" by Dobson)

Among the great men of historical
immigrant families were the explorers,
Lewis and Clark, the frontiersman Davy
Crockett, President Andrew Jackson, man of
the battle at the Alamo Sam Houston, and
our own John Caldwell Calhoun, of CLAN
COLQUHOUN, statesman extraordinaire and
others.

OPPORTUNITIES OF THE NEW WORLD

From the bonnie, bonnie banks of Loch Lomond and the environs of Ireland to the green, green valleys of the Shenandoah came the COLQUHOUNS along with many of their neighbors. The Plantation into Ireland though successful for a time soon was ineffectual. Some stayed and suffered the hardships there, but many came to America, the land of hope and expectation of fulfilled dreams.

Like the ripple of the sea when a stone is tossed, the COLQUHOUNS multiplied and scattered over the entire nation and into the world. By then many had adopted different spellings of their name omitting the "qu", feeling that the shortened form would be better suited for a new life style in the lately acquired homeland of their choice.

From John, William and Patrick, the three brothers who came to the U. S. in 1733, this group of people spread like wild fire in a parched field. Genealogical charts prepared by scholars of family history have shown that they were progenitors of the kindred CALHOUNS who were directly descended from them.

PATRICK AND CATHERINE MONTGOMERY CALHOUN, were immigrants to Lancaster PA in 1733. They were born in Londonderry, Ireland, and moved from Donegal County, Ireland before sailing to America. Their children: Mary, William, Ezekiel, James and Patrick,

Jr. are identified as the ancestors of the largest group of descendents available for inclusion in the book "American Born Descendents of the COLQUHOUNS of Scotland".

PATRICK, JR. was the father of JOHN CALDWELL CALHOUN, probably the best known CALHOUN of American heritage. He stated that PATRICK CALHOUN, JR. from Londonderry, Ireland was his father. JCC was born near Abbeville, SC on March 18, 1782. His father was a slave-holding farmer who died when JCC was fourteen years old. He was sixteen when his mother died, thus leaving him to fend for himself on the farm doing hard manual labor.

Some of CALHOUN's relatives recognized the potential in this bright and ambitious young man and enabled him to be educated at Moses Waddell's Log College in Georgia, Yale University and law studies under Tapping Reeve at Litchfield, Conn. His admission to the South Carolina Bar in Charleston and Abbeville in 1807 started a promising political career which was a dream come true though never expected.

JOHN CALDWELL CALHOUN distinguished himself as statesman and political philosopher. His lifetime contribution to the new world made his name famous and made those of his kin proud that he was one of them.

His countenance was that of a distinguished southern gentleman with

flowing white hair not quite shoulder
length and sparkling blue eyes. His
handsome looks and demeanor was attractive
to the ladies. He chose as his life long
companion, Floride Calhoun and on January
8, 1811 they were married. She, the
daughter of John Ewing COLHOUN, died July
25, 1866.

JOHN C. CALHOUN was a champion of southern
rights and while serving as South Carolina
State Legislator in 1808 was considered a
prominent War Hawk urging war with England
to vindicate American honor. His stand
on States Rights made him popular with
the people who were solidly behind his
desire to be a Congressman. He was
elected with an overwhelming victory.
After a short time he was appointed as
acting head of the Foreign Relations
Committee, a position he held until 1816.

Then, he was appointed Secretary of War in
President Monroe's Cabinet supporting the
American system which called for a tariff
to promote commerce and industry through
federally financed infrastructure. His
ambition to become President of the US led
him to resign his post as Secretary of War
in 1824. CALHOUN was disappointed to lose
the election to Andrew Jackson, but he
was elected Vice-President of the USA to
serve with Andrew Jackson, as President.

Perhaps his disassociation from the States
Rights position advocated by southern
conservatives was responsible for his
defeat as President. The enormity of

144

cotton cultivation and production in the
south which was dependent on slavery led
him to believe that with federal backing
of industry and commerce the interests of
the south could no longer be sustained.

Though reelected VP in 1828, his effort to
dominate the Jackson organization was
frustrated by Jackson's refusal to endorse
an extremist position on States Rights.
CALHOUN had taken other actions contrary
to Jackson thus creating friction and in
1832 resigned. He was then elected as US
Senator from South Carolina, a position he
kept until 1843. Then he served only a
year as Secretary of State in President
Tyler's cabinet. During this time CALHOUN
engineered the controversial annexation of
Texas.

Again in 1845-50 he was appointed
Secretary of State. The rest of his life
was spent defending the right of slavery
to expand into the remainder of the USA.
He predicted that if this was not done
that states would secede from the Union.
History tells us that he was correct but
he held a firm belief in the rights of the
south as a minority region. His death on
March 31, 1850 ended a brilliant career
unequalled in service to his country by
anyone of that day.

Fort Hill in the Senaca River valley in
SC, was named "Clergy Hall" when built in
1803 by Rev. James McIlhaney to
memorialize a fort which was there in
1776. It became the family home when

JOHN CALDWELL CALHOUN purchased it in 1824 and moved his family there. At his death a controversy over his will began and was finally settled by the court with his second daughter, Anna Maria CALHOUN who married Colonel Thomas Green Clemson on November 13, 1838,acquiring the homestead. She donated the land and all the surrounding land to South Carolina for a farming and mechanical college which was named Clemson University. It is standing today as a monument to this great American who was one of us. The COLQUHOUN/CALHOUN family reunion is held there periodically.

Though the career of this JOHN CALDWELL CALHOUN was the most spectacular and rewarding to family history, other members were well received in this new country and made their own niche in the fabric and weave of the civilization. Many CALHOUN, CAHOON, COHOON, COLHOUN people with varied other spelling of their names soon forgot the association of their connecting threads to the COLQUHOUNS from the western banks of Loch Lomond while forging a new life for themselves.

Some few fiercely proud people continued the use of COLQUHOUN even to the point that if other's names weren't spelled as the original, they claimed no kin to them.

These people using the Scottish name scattered to many places in the world. A friend from California told me that she was visiting in Australia and noticed a name tag with the surname, COLQUHOUN. In

146

their conversation she told them that she had a friend back home who used the same spelling and was informed that there were quite a number of them in Australia. California telephone books contain listings for these brave people who insist on using the ancestral spelling.

COLQUHOUN/CALHOUN

JAMES, EZEKIEL, WILLIAM, PATRICK AND OTHERS

Those immigrants moving into the new world came expecting land grants which were offered on a first come first serve basis. When there was not available land grant acreage suitable to their purpose, they either bought what they wanted or moved to more fertile pastures where water was available and the land arable.

The four sons and one daughter of PATRICK CALHOUN and Catherine Montgomery, who, after a arduous trip of many weeks aboard ship in 1733, according to recorded data were found farming in Lancaster County, PA where Patrick, Sr. died in 1741. Records of his will have been found in Lancaster, PA with probate from 1741-1744.

William remained in PA in what was named Dauphin, a portion of Lancaster County until 1785. His will dated August 1, 1748 provided the following grants to his sons, William CALHOUN 150 acres on October 30, 1765, James 300 acres on February 20, 1770 and to George 150 acres on May 16, 1748.

No doubt the family travelled by horseback and wagons down the Shenandoah Valley bringing them to Wythe County, Virginia. County records show that after specific services had been performed in that area by the Calhoun family for a period of approximately ten years, they

148

moved in a group to what is now Abbeville
County, South Carolina in February 1756.

Building their new and permanent log home
at the fork of two rivers in CALHOUN
Settlement on Long Cane Creek seemed to be
the most suitable place where they felt
safe from the Cherokee Indians who were
sixteen miles away.They had fled Virginia
because there was no protection from the
Indian attacks which became regular and
unprovoked. This spot in the wilderness
seemed ideal with wild game being rampant.

In their new home they still were not safe
from the Cherokees who raided their
property, killed the women and children
and generally made life miserable. It was
during one of these raids that the lives
of CATHERINE MONTGOMERY CALHOUN and her
son, James, along with twenty-one others
were taken. It was in February, 1760 when
the Long Cane Massacre took place.

Some of the CALHOUNS fleeing to Augusta,
Georgia for protection with their
belongings in thirteen wagons were
accosted by Indians on the trail. Records
indicate that approximately two hundred
and fifty people were in flight with some
fifty of them brutally murdered. PATRICK
returned to Long Cane Creek to assess the
damage done to their houses and erect
tombstones to memorialize those dead. Some
of the CALHOUNS moved back to their
homes on Long Cane Creek, SC in later
years and some found safer lands for their
homestead.

The CALHOUNS with brothers and cousins had claimed public lands for their homes with surveys done by PATRICK, III, the youngest son of PATRICK, JR. and Catherine CALHOUN. He was given his headright (homestead) for his services.

MARY CATHERINE CALHOUN, the only daughter, arrived in the new country with her parents, her husband John Noble and their son, James Noble. Some genealogists claim that after the journey aboard ship they landed in the Port of New York. Preponderance of evidence from written records disputes the claim. Others insist that their landing was at the port in Philadelphia, PA.

EZEKIEL, second son of PATRICK, SR. and CATHERINE CALHOUN, was appointed supervisor of road work done in VA around the Wood's River area. He moved with his family to Long Cane Creek settlement where he lived until his death. His will was recorded in Charleston, SC on May 25, 1762 leaving property equally divided to his wife, Jean and children, Jeanne, Rebecca, John Ewing, Catherine, Mary, Patrick and Ezekiel.

Family diaries were kept describing the condition of the times. These people though farmers and working class were educated to varying degrees. Thus the genealogical records have survived the years, been reproduced, and read by kin and others alike. There are so many with

150

the names of Patrick, James, John, Robert,
William and others that have been given to
newborns from the times in Scotland until
today that trying to determine who is a
particular son of a particular father is
not an easy task.

By the end of the nineteenth century the
family that originated in Scotland on the
western bank of Loch Lomond was listed in
almost every state with eighty-five
percent of the CALHOUNS coming from the
four brothers with PATRICK SR. and
Catherine in 1733. Our branch of the
COLQUHOUN CLAN came from the Camstradden
area and were evidently from the fifteen
percent of the CLAN not connected to
PATRICK AND CATHERINE yet they are proven
descendents of UMFRIDUS FIRST OF
COLQUHOUN.

Family records in my great grandmother's
handwriting do not give birth place nor
dates for those in the preceding years
prior to MARTHA ANN COLQUHOUN. Only a few
things are known about them. There were
two sets of twins named Robert and James.
One James married Martha Gatewood. There
is no indication that they lived in the
US since some of the family record states
that JAMES COLQUHOUN who married Mary
Francis Sulivan, my great grandmother, was
from Scotland. There are many, many James
names in the census records of the Family
History Center IGI, but none with the
birthday of 1809 that is his.

COLQUHOUN/CALHOUN

JAMES AND MARY FRANCIS were married in Danville, VA and moved to Madison County, MS where several of their children were born. They are also buried in Madison County, MS. Grandmother MARTHA ANN COLQUHOUN was married in Brandon, Ms to CAPTAIN JAMES MASON RANDEL.

A few facts were learned from ROBERT COLQUHOUN RANDEL at his knees before the fireplace on a cold winter's night.There were several COLQUHOUN red heads with fair complexion which Dad always said was the demeanor of a true Scotsman. The typical COLQUHOUN had auburn hair, very deep set blue eyes and bushy eyebrows. Their stamina was great though some were very egotistical and appreciated flattery.

Many of them had musical talents which is evident still in COLQUHOUN descendents today. Bagpipes, violin, piano, banjo, and solo voices have all been talents of theirs through the ages.

Dreams of a young girl and her parent at fireside chats were of a future of riches from a lawsuit due from French Spoilation Claims. The following letter is self-explanatory.

"Office of Ludovic C. Cleemann,
Attorney At Law
16 South Third St.
Philadelphia,
May 15, 1886

"Dear Sir,   (My, grandfather, JAMES MASON RANDEL)
I learn from correspondence you have had with my brother Thomas M. Cleemann that you married a daughter of Mr. JAMES COLQUHOUN of Mississippi. This Mr. JAMES COLQUHOUN was a nephew of Mr. ROBERT COLQUHOUN who was in business with his cousin, Mr. WALTER COLQUHOUN under the firm name of ROBERT AND WALTER COLQUHOUN in the latter part of the last century in Petersburg, Virginia.

They lost two cargoes of tobacco by capture by French privateers and their heirs have a claim against the United States Government for a portion of the lost cargo from the French Spoilations Act and the underwriters in London, our claim being chiefly to recover back the premium on the insurance which they had to pay, which was very high amounting to from $35,000 to $40,000.

Because at this great distance of time, the captures having been made in the year 1798, proof of value will be hard to obtain. Still we ought to make the effort to prove the claims and if you will send me the information asked for above, I will insert it in my petition and your branch of the family will stand right upon the record.

Mr. JAMES COLQUHOUN's descendents, if my genealogy is correct, would receive between them one fourth of the whole amount recovered. That is if upon the

theory that ROBERT COLQUHOUN left but two
brothers, one JAMES COLQUHOUN, your wife's
grandfather, and one WILLIAM COLQUHOUN who
lived in Scotland.

What I need to know is whether Mr. JAMES
COLQUHOUN is still alive. If not, I then
wish this further information. Did he
leave a will and if a will, what its
provisions are: or if he died intestate,
did he leave a widow and is she living and
what are the names and relationship of
those who survived him and became entitled
to his estate. And if any of those who
inherited from him are now dead whether
they died intestate, married or unmarried
and the names of their wives or husbands
and of their children.

Whether we can recover any thing on these
claims is doubtful for several reasons:
1: Because Congress only allows us to
prove our claims but has made no provision
for their payment.
2: Because both Congresses were insured
against war risks. An act passed Congress
allowing claimants to prove their claims
before the Court of Claims at Washington,
such claims to be presented within two
years from January 1885. Mrs. J. C.
Pannill, a lineal descendent of WALTER
COLQUHOUN, residing in Petersburg,
Virginia has taken out a letter of
Administration in the Estates of ROBERT
AND WALTER COLQUHOUN, and as her counsel I
am going to make an effort to prove the
claims before the Court of claims, I,
being an attorney of that court and also

one of the lineal descendants of WALTER
COLQUHOUN. The rules of the Court of
Claims seem to require that the names of
all persons interested should be inserted
in the petition and I write this to you
for information concerning Mr. JAMES
COLQUHOUN, as I know, as stated above,
that you once corresponded on the subject
of family matters with my brother, Thos.
M. Cleemann. ....had an only child a
daughter, who died, as we believe,
unmarried and without issue. If any of
this Scot WILLIAM COLQUHOUN's descendents
are living or even if he made a will, it
might diminish your wife's share. Hoping
you may be able at an early day to give me
the information desired above.

Believe me
Very truly yours,"

L. C. Cleemann.

Not being privileged to have the response
from my grandfather to Attorney Cleemann,
we do not have all of the family
information that we might have for the
genealogical record. The ROBERT mentioned
was one of the twins born in the mid-
1700s. WALTER, a son of LUDOWICK AND
CHRISTIAN MCLELLAN COLQUHOUN, was a cousin
to ROBERT.

Several letters followed in 1886, in 1894
and 1897. All said virtually the same
thing. The Court's action on all of the
French Spoilations Claims seemed to
sidestep the problem, requiring proof of
the ownership of the cargo (100 years

later) and sending the matter to the Supreme Court.

Cleemann stressed the fact that the claim was merely for the Insurance premiums paid to the Underwriters in London. The US Government did not receive those payments and thus was not claiming responsibility. He stated that since the US Government did not protect the commerce of its citizens, the Messrs. COLQUHOUN were forced to insure against the risk of capture, an expense they would not have been put to had the US Government done its duty.

In 1894 Cleemann said that due to the present depleted state of the U. S. treasury, it is almost certain that even if a decision was ordered in favor of the claims in the Court, Congress would not make an appropriation to pay them even though some of the claims to others who had been successful in their suits three years ago (1891) have been paid. Our family never received as Dad said, "A red copper cent."

As we pondered this by the fire in 1920-25, Daddy computed interest at the going rate and divided the spoils by all of the living heirs. On the back of one of the letters his figures show amount of $8,256 due his family.

A picture of the S. S. CLAN COLQUHOUN Liner (1899) gave evidence that Robert Hazlitt COLQUHOUN 1785/1875 and Charles

COLQUHOUN/CALHOUN

Alexander COLHOUN 1822/ were living in
Montgomery Co., Christiansburg, VA.

Though relatives of ROBERT COLQUHOUN
RANDEL may have changed their names,
all of those whom he knew were still using
the name with "qu" intact. His mother,
MARTHA ANN COLQUHOUN, was in a wheel chair
for the last part of her life.
Presumption is that she wrote a very
poignant poem which expressed her feelings
at that time. It may have been one that
was anonymous which touched her so much
that she copied it down. We'll never know.

WEARY THE WAITING

There's an end to all toiling some day.
But its weary the waiting--weary!
There's a harbor somewhere in a peaceful
bay
Where the sails will be furled and ships
will stay
At anchor--somewhere far away.
But its weary the waiting- weary!

There's an end to the troubles of souls
oppressed.
But its weary the waiting -- weary!
Sometimes in the future when God thinks
best,
He'll lay us down tenderly to rest.
And roses will grow from the thorns in the
breast.
But its weary the waiting--weary!

There's an end to the world with its
stormy frown.

157

COLQUHOUN/CALHOUN

But its weary the waiting--weary!
There's a light somewhere that no dark can
        drown
And where life's sad burdens are all laid
        down
A crown- thank God- for each crop a crown!
But its weary the waiting--weary!

                MAMA

A P P E N D I X

DEFINITIONS

BIRTHS/DEATHS	AS:	1715/1790
BIRTHS/	AS:	1715/
DEATHS/	AS:	/1790
CA	AS:	AROUND, APPROXIMATELY
D/O	AS:	DAUGHTER OF
F	AS:	FEMALE
H/O	AS:	HUSBAND OF
M/	AS:	MARRIED
(NN)	AS:	NO NAME
S/	AS:	SINGLE
S/O	AS:	SON OF
W/O	AS:	WIFE OF
W/	AS:	WITH

OTHER DATES SELF EXPLANATORY
THOSE WITH NO DATES LISTED LAST

INDIVIDUALS AND FAMILIES
IN SCOTLAND AND IRELAND

Umfridus de Kilpatrick and de COLQUHOUN 1190/1260 Dumbarton, Scotland, the first documented Chief of COLQUHOUN, m/ to a COLQUHOUN related to Luss.

Sir Robert 2nd de COLQUHOUN 1220/1280 Scotland, s/o Umfridus de COLQUHOUN.

Ingleramus 3rd de COLQUHOUN 1250/ 1308, Dumbarton, Scotland s/o Sir Robert 2nd.

Sir Humphrey 4th of COLQUHOUN 1280/1330, Dumbarton, Scotland s/o Ingleramus 3rd of COLQUHOUN.

Sir Robert 5th de COLQUHOUN and 7th of Luss 1310/1390, Dumbarton, Scotland.

Sir Humphrey 6th of COLQUHOUN and 8th of Luss 1345/1406, Dumbarton, Scotland s/o Robert 5th of COLQUHOUN and 8th of Luss.

Robert COLQUHOUN 1346/1429 Scotland, Camstradden the Branch from which ROBERT COLQUHOUN RANDEL descends.

Sir Robert 7th of COLQUHOUN and 9th of Luss 1368/1408 Scotland, second s/o Sir Humphrey 6th of COLQUHOUN and 8th of Luss.

Sir John 8th of COLQUHOUN and 10th of Luss 1370/1439, Dumbarton, Scotland m/Jean Erskine, d/o Lord Robert Erskine.

160

COLQUHOUN/CALHOUN (APPENDIX)

Mary COLQUHOUN 1375/1456, Renfrew, Scotland m/ to Sir Patrick Houstan /1450.

Christian COLQUHOUN 1375/ Glengarnock, Scotland, m/ to James Cunningham.

Malcolm COLQUHOUN 1395/ 1440, Dumbarton, Scotland wife unknown, their son, John.

Sir John 9th of COLQUHOUN and 11th of Luss 1420/1478, Dumbarton, Scotland died at Dunbar in battle, m/ 1st Lady Boyd and 2nd to Lady Elizabeth Dunbar.

Sir Humphrey 10th of COLQUHOUN and 12th of Luss 1440/1493,Dumbarton, Scotland m/ Lady Jean Erskine d/o Lord Thomas Erskine, 2nd Marion Baillie.

Sir John 11th of COLQUHOUN & 13th of Luss 1475/1536, Dumbarton, Scotland m/1st Lady Elizabeth (Margaret Stuart) and second Margaret Cunningham d/o William Cunningham.

Sir Humphrey 12th of COLQUHOUN & 14th of Luss 1495/1557,Dumbarton, Scotland m/ Lady Catherine Graham d/o William Graham 1st Earl of Montrose.

Walter COLQUHOUN 1500/, Craigton, Scotland ancestor of the COLQUHOUNS of Kilmardinny.

Rev. John COLQUHOUN 1511/1570,Glasgow Scotland.

Marion COLQUHOUN 1513/, Glasgow Scotland m/ Sir Robert Boyd.

COLQUHOUN/CALHOUN (APPENDIX)

Marjory COLQUHOUN 1513,Glenurchy, Scotland
m/ Sir Duncan Campbell.

Sir John 13th of COLQUHOUN and 15th
of Luss 1515/1574, Dumbarton, Scotland
m/1st Lady Christian Erskine; 2nd Lady
Agnes Boyd.

Catherine COLQUHOUN 1516/ Arrochar,
Scotland m/ to Duncan MacFarlane.

James COLQUHOUN 1517/, Garscube, Scotland
m/ to Christian Campbell Oct.28,1558.

Patrick COLQUHOUN 1519/ Dumbarton,
Scotland m/ Janet Murray, sister of John
of Strowan.

Adam COLQUHOUN 1520/ Stobo, Scotland was
Rector of Stobo Church.

Helen COLQUHOUN 1523/ Aiket, Scotland m/
James Cunningham.

Marion COLQUHOUN 1525/, Ardkinlass,
Scotland m/ Colin Campbell.

Giles COLQUHOUN 1526/ Luss, Scotland m/
William Chirnside.

Agnes Boyd 1540/1584, Edinburgh,Scotland
m/ Sir John 13th of COLQUHOUN and 15th of
Luss.

Sir Humphrey 14th of COLQUHOUN and 16th of
Luss 1565/1592, Luss, Scotland m/1st Lady
Jean Cunningham d/ of Alexander Earl of

162

Glencairn and 2nd Lady Jean Hamilton d/o Lord John Hamilton.

John Roy COLQUHOUN 1567/1592, Edinburgh, Scotland was beheaded for killing his brother, Sir Humphrey 14th of COLQUHOUN.

Jean COLQUHOUN 1569/, Glasgow, Scotland , lived in Minto, Scotland briefly m/ Sir Matthew Stuart.

Sir Alexander COLQUHOUN 1573/1617 Luss, Scotland, m/ Helen Buchanan.

Margaret COLQUHOUN 1574/, Duntreath, Scotland,m/Sir James Edmonstone, Knight.

Anna COLQUHOUN 1588/, Edinburgh, Scotland m/ Colin Campbell.

Sir John 16th of COLQUHOUN and 18th of Luss 1596/1676, Luss, Scotland, m/ Lady Lillian (Lillias) Graham and 2nd Lady Katherine Graham.

Adam COLQUHOUN 1601/1634, Dumbarton, Scotland m/ Lady Christian Lindsay of Bonniel, Scotland.

Adam COLQUHOUN 1601/Ireland s/o Sir Alexander 15th of COLQUHOUN and 17th of Luss m/ d/o Lindsey of Bonhill.

Alexander COLQUHOUN 1601/ Dumbarton, Scotland s/o Adam COLQUHOUN, married Margaret Helen Buchanan. Had son named Adam COLQUHOUN.

COLQUHOUN/CALHOUN (APPENDIX)

George COLQUHOUN 1603/ Sweden, brother
Walter changed name to Cahun, Gahn, etc.

Jean COLQUHOUN 1605/, Abercorn, Scotland.
Jean m/1st Lord Allan Cathcart 5th Baron,
2nd Sir Duncan Campbell of Auchinbreck,
3rd Sir William Hamilton s/o James.

Nancy (Nans) COLQUHOUN 1606/ Corkagh Co.,
Donegal, Ireland m/ John McAnselan.

Catherine COLQUHOUN 1607/ Scotland, m/ Sir
John Mure.

Humphrey COLQUHOUN 1618/ Balvie, Scotland,
m/ Margaret Somerville.

Sir Alexander 17th COLQUHOUN of
Tullichewan 1619/, Tullichewan, Scotland
m/ Marion Stirling.

Walter COLQUHOUN 1620/ Sweden cannon-
founder- wife unknown- many children.

Sir James Alexander COLQUHOUN of
Tullychewen 1621/ Scotland, (Tillyquhoun
COLQUHOUNS of Tillyquhoun descend from
him) m/Anabella Stewart, d/o Archibald
Stewart.

Sir John 17th of COLQUHOUN and 19th of
Luss 1621/, Dumbarton, Scotland m/ 1636
Margaret Baillie d/o Lochend, Baronet,2nd
Margaret d/o Lord David.

Robert COLQUHOUN 1622/ s/o of Adam m/
Katherine MacCausland, his first cousin.

COLQUHOUN/CALHOUN (APPENDIX)

Jean COLQUHOUN 1630/ m/   Walter Stewart.

Lillas COLQUHOUN 1631/,Dumbarton, Scotland
m/ John Napier s/o Robert of Killaman.

Catherine COLQUHOUN /1633 Dumbarton,
Scotland m/John Drummond.

William Cohoon 1633 in Tullichewan,
Scotland/6,22,1675 in Rehoboth, MA came
from Scotland to Taunton, Mass in 1635
m/Deliverence Peck and moved to Block
Island. Children: Samuel 1663/ Block
Island/ m/Mary Hunter 1698; Mary 1664/ m/
Thomas Jones; Joseph 1665/ m/ Hannah Kent;
William 1669/drowned 1696 m/1690 Elizabeth
Nickerson; James 2,15,1671/1747 Delaware
m/ Mary Cleghorn-Davis; Captain John
3,9,1673/ m/ Comfort Peet; Nathaniel
2,2,1675 m/ Janet Jones 1702.

William Cahoon m/ Elizabeth (NN) Children:
John   1691/;   Mary   1692/   Elizabeth
1694/1784; William 1695/1768 in Harwich,
MA m/1716 Sarah O'Killey; James 1696/
m/8,29,1722 to Mary Rich. Some of the
sons went to Barbados. Brothers with
William to USA were Archibald and Angus.

Sir James 19th of COLQUHOUN and 21st of
Luss 4th Baronet of Nova Scotia 1640/1688
Dumbarton, Scotland m/ 1659 Penuel
Cunningham, co-heiress of William of
Ballyachen, Donegal Ireland.

COLQUHOUN/CALHOUN (APPENDIX)

William COLQUHOUN 1643/,   Newton-Stewart
County of Tyrone, Ireland   s/o   Robert
1622/ m/ Catherine MacCauseland 1643/.

Sir Humphrey 20th of COLQUHOUN and 22nd of
Luss 1660/1718 (Rossdhu) Luss,Scotland m/
Margaret Houston d/o Patrick of that ILK.
Passed heirship to daughter Anne COLQUHOUN
through her husband, James Grant.

Rev. Alexander COLQUHOUN 1662/ Ireland s/o
William COLQUHOUN 1643/.

Sir James COLQUHOUN 3rd Baronet of Nova
Scotia (Minor) 1676 /1680   Dumbarton,
Scotland,   died without issue.   Uncle
James 19th of COLQUHOUN succeeded him.

James Grant of Pluscardine 6th Baronet of
Luss 1679/1747 h/o   Anne COLQUHOUN, d/o
Sir Humphrey 20th of COLQUHOUN.

Patrick   COLQUHOUN I USA m/Catherine
Montgomery   1683/   in   Londonderry,
N.Ireland emigrant   from   Ireland   to
Lancaster Co. PA in 1733. Children: Mary,
James, Ezekiel, William, and Patrick, Jr.

James Patrick COLQUHOUN 1686/ USA brother
of John, Alexander, Audley and William all
came to US in 1733 s/o Alexander 1662/.

William COLQUHOUN 1686/   Ireland   f/o
Patrick I immigrant from   Ireland   to
Pennsylvania in 1733   s/o   Rev.   Alex
COLQUHOUN 1662/ Newton-Stewart, Tyrone Co.
Ireland.

COLQUHOUN/CALHOUN (APPENDIX)

Patrick COLQUHOUN 1690/ Cardross, Dumbarton, daughter Agnes, m/ Mary McNeil.

Humphrey Grant s/o Anne COLQUHOUN 1700/1752 Luss,Scotland died without issue and title passed to Sir Ludovick COLQUHOUN, 7th Baronet.

Sir Ludovick 22nd of COLQUHOUN and 24th of Luss, 7th Baronet 1701/1732 Luss,Scotland, Title passed to brother James.

Alexander Grant 1709/1712 Luss,Scotland son of James and Anne COLQUHOUN.

Adam COLQUHOUN 1714/ Dumbarton, Scotland Father Patrick COLQUHOUN m/Agnes McNair.

Mary Catherine COLQUHOUN 1714/, Pennsylvania, USA d/o Patrick COLQUHOUN I & Catherine Montgomery m/ 1730 to John Noble.

Archibald COLQUHOUN, 1715/ a farmer, Jacobite, residence Appin Argyll, came from Tilbury on March 20, 1747 to Jamaica or Barbados on the St. George or Carteret (ships).

James COLQUHOUN 1716/1760 was second child of Patrick Calhoun (COLQUHOUN) and Catherine Montgomery born in Donegal, N. Ireland m/ Nancy Ann (Susannah) Long 1736. Came to Augusta, VA. Their son James, Jr.

Francis Grant 1717/ Luss, Scotland,

COLQUHOUN/CALHOUN (APPENDIX)

s/o James and Anne m/ a lady whose surname was Cox.

John COLQUHOUN 1717/ Dumbarton, Scotland, his son James. John possibly s/o Sir Humphrey 20th.

Lady Helen Sutherland COLQUHOUN 1717/1791 Rossdhu, Luss, Scotland, eldest d/o Lord William of Strathnaver.

Sir James 23rd of COLQUHOUN and 25th of Luss 1717/1786 Rossdhu, Luss, Scotland, m/ Lady Helen Sutherland in 1740.

Charles Cathart Grant 1723/ Luss,Scotland, son of James and Anne COLQUHOUN.

Patrick COLQUHOUN III 1737/ USA m/1st Alice Craighead and second Sarah McKinley, d/o James Calhoun and Nancy Ann Long.Scotland, died at Edinburgh. Buried Rossdhu m/Mary Falconer of Monktown 1773, youngest d/o James of Monktown.

William COLQUHOUN 1742/ Luss, Scotland, m/ Elizabeth Henderson.

Anne COLQUHOUN 1746/1748 Luss, Scotland.

Janet COLQUHOUN 1747/Scotland m/ General John Campbell of Barbreck 1766.

Margaret COLQUHOUN 1748/ Luss, Scotland, m/ William Baillie of Polkemet.

Catherine COLQUHOUN 1749/ Scotland m/ Sir MacKenzie, Baronet of Scatwell.

COLQUHOUN/CALHOUN (APPENDIX)

Alexander COLQUHOUN was surgeon in Edinburgh, Scotland before coming to New York in 1749.

Walter COLQUHOUN 1750/2,12,1802 came from Greenock to Antigua on the "Chance" and settled in Dominica and Antigua, married Elizabeth McAlister. Buried at St. John's Antigua.

Helen COLQUHOUN 1750/ Luss, Scotland, m/ William COLQUHOUN of Garscadden from Dumbarton, Scotland.

Jane COLQUHOUN 1751/ Fife, Scotland, m/ Evenezer Marsall Gardner of Hillcairiney Co., Fife.

Patrick COLQUHOUN 1751/ Edinburgh Parish, Edinburgh, Scotland D/O Agnes (NN) Midlothian, Scotland m/ Margaret Stewart.

Ludovick COLQUHOUN 1757/ Luss, Scotland, m/ Barbara Camilla/ d/o Rev. Dr. MacIntire.

James COLQUHOUN 1758/ m/ Jean Colquhoun.

Malcolm COLQUHOUN Jan. 28, 1764/ came from Skye to Virginia, 1792. Moved to MC 1810 m/ 1810 Christian McCorquodale (Q.V.).

James COLQUHOUN 1765/ Glasgow and Lanark, Scotland, m/ Christian.

COLQUHOUN/CALHOUN (APPENDIX)

Mary COLQUHOUN 1765/ in Scotland, m/ in Scotland in 1784 Archibald Alexander. f/o of Mary Archibald Alexander and Mary Christie Alexander.

Mary Falconer COLQUHOUN 1765/1833 Rossdhu, Annfield House, Fifeshire Luss, Scotland, m/ Sir James 24th of COLQUHOUN and 26th of Luss.

James COLQUHOUN 1766/, Luss, Scotland, Dumbarton, possible s/o Sir Humphrey and Agnes Collier.

James COLQUHOUN 1774/, Roseneath, Dumbarton, Scotland s/o James and Mary COLQUHOUN.

Sir James 25th of COLQUHOUN and 27th of Luss 1774/1836 Rossdhu Luss, Scotland, died in Edinburgh m/Janet Sinclair of Ulbster d/o Sir John Sinclair.

Agnes COLQUHOUN m/ Archibald in 1777.

Agnes COLQUHOUN 1779/ Dumbarton, Scotland d/o Patrick COLQUHOUN and Margaret COLQUHOUN.

John COLQUHOUN 1780/ Glasgow and Lanark, Scotland.

James COLQUHOUN 1781/ m/ Janet Hamilton.

James COLQUHOUN 1782/, Bonhill, Dumbarton.

COLQUHOUN/CALHOUN (APPENDIX)

John Campbell COLQUHOUN 1785/1854, Luss, Scotland.

Burgess Archibald COLQUHOUN /August 7, 1786. To USA from Dumbarton, Scotland s/o James COLQUHOUN who matriculated at Glasgow University, 1783. Came to Washington, North Carolina before 1786.

James COLQUHOUN 1788/, Abbey (Paisley) Renfrew, Scotland m/ Janet Hamilton.

Jane COLQUHOUN 1788/, Luss, Scotland, m/ David Kemp of Belsumset Lodge of County Fife, Scotland.

Walter C. COLQUHOUN 1788/ Rhu, Dumbarton, Scotland came to Hudson Bay, Ca 1813.

John COLQUHOUN 1790/, Glasgow, Lanark, Scotland m/ Euphan M'Kenzie.

William COLQUHOUN (Calhoun) 1796, came to Washington County, PA, USA in May 1818. Appeared on 1820 Census.

James COLQUHOUN 1797/, St. Luke Old St. Finsbury, London, England s/o Margaret COLQUHOUN.

Robert C. COLQUHOUN came from Glasgow on Merchant ship in St. Kitts during 1700S.

Dorothy Farley Cunningham 1802/, Davidson County, TN d/o Ann COLQUHOUN and William Cunningham Farley.

171

COLQUHOUN/CALHOUN (APPENDIX)

Helen COLQUHOUN 1804 Luss, Scotland m/
John Page Reade of Sutton House, Ipswich,
their son, John.

Sir James 26th of COLQUHOUN and 28th of
Luss 1804/1873 Luss, Scotland, drowned in
Loch Lomond m/ Jane Abercombie 2nd d/o Sir
Robert, Baronet of Birkenbob.

John COLQUHOUN 1805/ Luss, Scotland m/
Frances Sarah Maitland, 4th d/o Ebenezer
Fuller, Esq.

William COLQUHOUN 1806/ Luss, Scotland,
m/Sarah Maitland 1802/.

Robert COLQUHOUN 1808/, Glasgow, Lanark,
Scotland s/o Adam m/ to Janet Mason.

James COLQUHOUN, wife two sons and four
daughters came to Canada from Scotland on
Ship "Commerce" to Lanark Upper Canada on
October 1, 1820. Received land grant in
June, 1829.

Angus COLQUHOUN, immigrant from Scotland
with wife, son and three daughters came to
Canada on the ship "George Canning" in
June 1821. Received a Red land grant in
Lanark, Upper Canada in July 28, 1821.

James C. COLQUHOUN with wife, son, two
daughters came to Canada from Scotland on
the "George Canning". Received a land
grant in Lanark on July 25, 1821.

Archibald COLQUHOUN with wife, son, two
daughters came to Canada from Scotland and

172

received land grant Ramsey, Upper Canada on August 16, 1822.

Ann COLQUHOUN m/John Charles Walker December 27, 1839, Saint Nicholas, Aberdeen, Scotland.

Sir James 27th of COLQUHOUN and 29th of Luss 1844/1907 Luss, Scotland m/twice.

Andrew Sutherland COLQUHOUN July 29, 1847/ s/o John Colquhoun/Mary Mearns Saint Nicholas, Aberdeen, Scotland.

John COLQUHOUN 1853/ Scotland, Maybole, Ayr, Scotland.

James COLQUHOUN 1858/, High Church Paisley, Renfrew, Scotland m/Elizabeth Meiklejohn.

James Cahoon 1864/, 0857 Meigh, Armagh, Ireland m/ Bridget Morgan.

George Rodney COLQUHOUN 11,14,1865/ St Nicholas / s/o William COLQUHOUN and Ann Rodney.

Robert Colhoun 1867/ 0176 Londonderry, Ireland m/ Annie Walker.

Sir Alan 28th of COLQUHOUN and 30th of Luss 1895/1910 Luss, Scotland, 6th British Baronet m/ Justine Henrietta Kennedy of Underwood.

Sir Iain 29th of COLQUHOUN and 31st of Luss 1910/1948 Rossdhu, Scotland, was 7th

COLQUHOUN/CALHOUN (APPENDIX)

British   Baronet   m/Geraldine   Bryde
Tennant.

Sir Ivar 30th of COLQUHOUN and 32nd of
Luss 1920/, the current Chief m/ Kathleen
Duncan.

Alexander   COLQUHOUN   from   Edinburgh,
Scotland, was son of Alexander COLQUHOUN,
merchant to independent companies.

Alice Murthwaite COLQUHOUN born in Wales.
Lived in St. Croix.   Her daughter b/in
London, England.   Alice & two sisters
moved to Canada and to Mpls. MN

Margaret COLQUHOUN, w/o Hugh Crawford and
d/o Patrick COLQUHOUN and Isabel McCauley.
Hugh was born in Kilburne, Ayrshire
Scotland.

   THIS SECTION SORTED BY FIRST DATE
            IN PARAGRAPH

APPENDIX
INDIVIDUALS AND FAMILIES
IN AMERICA

BIRTHS/DEATHS

CALHOUN, Elbert Conley 10,10,1910/ 2,12,1956 (MS PFC HG. DET. STA.COM.WW2. He was a Mason and member of Order of Eastern Star). Buried in Calhoun Cemetery, Simpson, Co., MS.   *

CALHOUN, Hattie Ann 12,12,1873/ 11,4,1954 buried in Simpson Co., MS Calhoun Cemetery.   *

CALHOUN, J. A. 9,3,1866/ 12,23,1943 buried in Simpson Co., MS Calhoun Cemetery.*

CALHOUN, Levicie 2,25,1860/ m/12,20,1877 to A. A. Ponder /4/19/1891 buried in Simpson Co., MS. Calhoun Cemetery. *

CALHOUN, Lissie Ann 6,14,1879/1,21,1960 Calhoun Cemetery in Simpson Co. MS w/o William Marion CALHOUN.   *

CALHOUN, Mary M. 1,12,1868/ 11,2,1948 buried in Calhoun Cemetery in Simpson Co., Ms.   *

CALHOUN, Robert 9,17,1897/ m/Geneva Heckey His parents were David COLQUHOUN and Ann Bannatyne. Their children: Myrel CALHOUN m/M. S. Poulos; Jane CALHOUN m/ Alscot Power; Robert CALHOUN.

COLQUHOUN/CALHOUN

CALHOUN, William Marion 2,18,1876 /9,16,1955, Simpson Co. MS h/o Lissie Ann CALHOUN. Their infant son buried in CALHOUN Cemetery.   *

COLQUHOUN, Agnes 12,23,1781/ Scotland, d/o James COLQUHOUN and Janet Hamilton.

COLQUHOUN, Agnes 12,7,1782/ Bonhill, Dumbarton, Scotland, d/o James COLQUHOUN and Jean Ewing COLQUHOUN.

COLQUHOUN, Agnes 2,21,1805/ Glasgow and Lanark, Scotland d/o Robert COLQUHOUN and Janet Mason.

COLQUHOUN, Ann Talbot 11,24,1881/3,11,1958 Canada & Minnesota m/ Harry Cheadle Sanger.

COLQUHOUN, Arthur Hugh 1875/ Wales, Father Isaac COLQUHOUN.

COLQUHOUN, Carl David 12,11,1916/ m/6,27,37 Rosella Mae Johnson 6,23,1937/ His parents were James COLQUHOUN and Minnie Velin.

COLQUHOUN, Charles Gordon 9,14,1859/.

COLQUHOUN, Christian Noble (F) 7,25,1871/.

COLQUHOUN, Christibell COLQUHOUN 10,1834/ 11, 1834 d/o James and Mary Francis Sulivan COLQUHOUN.

COLQUHOUN/CALHOUN

COLQUHOUN, Ernest Cecil 1874/ Wales, Father Isaac COLQUHOUN.

COLQUHOUN, Estelle 4,3,1850/11,15,1887 d/o James and Mary Francis Sulivan COLQUHOUN.

COLQUHOUN, George 12,28,1910/ 3,25,1911 s/o R. N. and M. C. COLQUHOUN. Buried in CALHOUN Cemetery Simpson Co., MS *

COLQUHOUN, George Rodney 11,14,1865/

COLQUHOUN, Hortense 5,17,1854/3,19,1878 was buried in St. Louis Cemetery in New Orleans, LA. (An above ground cemetery). She d/o James and Mary Francis Sulivan COLQUHOUN.

COLQUHOUN, James 1,7,1797/ St. Luke Old St. Finsbury, London, England s/o Margaret COLQUHOUN.

COLQUHOUN, James 4,7,1765/ Glasgow and Lanark Scotland s/o Robert COLQUHOUN.

COLQUHOUN, James 4,24,1788/ in Abbey (Paisley) Renfrew, Scotland.

COLQUHOUN, James D. 6,14,1830/ twin to Robert N. s/o James and Mary Francis Sulivan COLQUHOUN.

COLQUHOUN, James 4,18,1774, Roseneath, Dumbarton, Scotland, s/o James and Mary COLQUHOUN.

COLQUHOUN/CALHOUN

COLQUHOUN, James 4,18,1774/ Roseneath, Dumbarton, Scotland s/o James and Mary COLQUHOUN.

COLQUHOUN, James 5,30,1891/5,25,1986 m/Minnie Velin 10,17,1888/3,25,1961. His parents were David COLQUHOUN and Anne Bannatyne. Their children were: Carl David COLQUHOUN 12,11,1916 m/Marie Iverson; Willard James COLQUHOUN 2,24,1921 m/Helen Nicatara.

COLQUHOUN, John 6,1,1827/ 12,14,1909 buried in Calhoun Cemetery, Simpson Co., MS.

COLQUHOUN, John 2,10,1870/ Glasgow, and Lanark, Scotland.

COLQUHOUN, John 12,23,1853/ Maybole, Ayr, Scotland.

COLQUHOUN, John 5,12,1717/ in Luss, Dumbarton, Scotland, son of James COLQUHOUN.

COLQUHOUN, John 6,23,1864/ Greenock, Renfrew Co., Scotland m/Lil. s/o Samuel COLQUHOUN and Rebecca Wilson. Their children: Reginald, Emilie, Muriel, and John Talbot, all COLQUHOUNS.

COLQUHOUN, Lucy Lee 4,25,1848/ 7,1858 d/o James COLQUHOUN and Mary Francis Sulivan COLQUHOUN.

COLQUHOUN, Ludvic 3,11,1854/2,8,1864 s/o James and Mary Francis Sulivan COLQUHOUN.

COLQUHOUN/CALHOUN

COLQUHOUN, Mary A. 10,15,1835/ 12/11/1884 in Simpson Co., MS Calhoun Cemetery. *

COLQUHOUN, Mary Balfour 8,1,1849/3,7,1883, w/o Charles C. Balfour. d/o James and Mary Francis Sulivan COLQUHOUN.

COLQUHOUN, Marion 1518/ Father John Iain COLQUHOUN.

COLQUHOUN, Mary Morrison, d/o John COLQUHOUN and Mary Mearns, 5,3,1853

COLQUHOUN, Patrick 1604/ Scotland, s/o Alexander COLQUHOUN.

COLQUHOUN, Peter Ludovic 1776/ s/o James COLQUHOUN.

COLQUHOUN, Robert 1332/s/o Robert COLQUHOUN.

COLQUHOUN, Robert 1356/ s/o Humphrey COLQUHOUN.

COLQUHOUN, Robert 1452/ s/o John COLQUHOUN.

COLQUHOUN, Sir Robert David 1786/ Scotland s/o George COLQUHOUN

COLQUHOUN, Rodney 10,12,1862/

COLQUHOUN, Sally, buried /5,9,1912 in Glenwood Cemetery, Canton, MS on the west side near the front of Cemetery.

COLQUHOUN, Samuel Scotland/ m/Rebecca Wilson. Their children: David COLQUHOUN 11,12,1852/10,29,1908 m/ Ann Bannatyne.

COLQUHOUN,Sarah Emeline2,8,1843/5,10,1916. d/o James COLQUHOUN and Mary Francis Sulivan COLQUHOUN.

COLQUHOUN, Sarah Maitland 1802/, Scotland d/o James COLQUHOUN.

COLQUHOUN, Sulivan 12,1859/1863 s/o James and Mary Francis Sulivan COLQUHOUN.

COLQUHOUN, Walter 1482/ Scotland father Humphrey COLQUHOUN.

COLQUHOUN, Walter 1514/ Scotland father John Iain COLQUHOUN.

COLQUHOUN, Walter 1602/ Scotland father Alexander.

COLQUHOUN, Walter 4,11,1840/ 8,23,1916 s/o James and Mary Francis Sulivan COLQUHOUN.

COLQUHOUN, WILLIAM 1686/ s/o Rev. Alexander COLQUHOUN 1662/ and Judith Hamilton d/o James Hamilton.

COLQUHOUN, William 1643/ of Newton-Stewart County, Tyron, Ireland m/ Catherine Mac Causeland.

COLQUHOUN, William 1806/ Scotland, s/o James COLQUHOUN.

COLQUHOUN/CALHOUN

COLQUHOUN, William Hanson 1807/ Scotland, s/o Frederick COLQUHOUN.

COLQUHOUN, William H. Shelton 7,4,1837/ 7,15,1837 s/o James and Mary Francis Sulivan COLQUHOUN.

COLQUHOUN, William Robert 1841/ spouse Frances Horton.

COLQUHOUN,Zula Mae 1909/ 3,15,1911, d/o R. N. and M. C. COLQUHOUN, buried in Calhoun Cemetery in Simpson Co., MS *.

COLQUOUN, Ann Evans 1844/ Wales, d/o James COLQUHOUN.

(* Calhoun Cemetery in Simpson Co., MS is located on Cato-Mendenhall Road between Cato and Bethany Methodist Church.)

CENSUS

CAHOON, Samuel, Nansemond Co., VA in 1783 w/7 whites and 15 blacks. In 1784 he was still in Nansemond, Co., VA w/7 whites, 1 dwelling, and 6 other buildings.

COLHOUN, Robert 8,17,1867/ in Londonderry, Ireland, spouse Annie Walker.

COLQUHAUN, John Cumberland Co., NC District 038 01 11 03 00 000

COLQUHAUN, John, Cumberland Co., NC William's District 258 1810.

181

COLQUHOUN/CALHOUN

COLQUEHOUN, Archibald, Rutherford Co., NC 1810.

COLQUEHORME, Archibald, Sampson Co. NC District 495 200010 31010 11 1800.

COLQUOHON, Charles, Richmond Co., NC No twp 1795

COLQUOHON, John, Richmond Co., NC No twp 1795.

COLQUHOUN, John, Cumberland Co., NC Black's District 251 1810.

COLQUHOON, Archebald Cumberland Co., NC District 038 01 00 03 00 00 1790

COLQUHOON, Duncan, Cumberland Co., NC District 038 01 00 01 00 00 1790

COLQUHOON, John, Cumberland Co., NC District 038 01 00 01 00 00 1790

COLQUHOON, Laughlan, Cumberland Co., NC District 038 01 02 04 00 00 1790

COLQUHOON, Malcolm, Cumberland Co., NC District 038 01 01 03 00 00 1790

COLQUHOON, Mrs., Cumberland, NC District 038 00 00 02 00 00 1790

COLQUHOUN, John, Cumberland Co., NC Black's District 251 1810

COLQUHOUN, Rebecca, Scotland, Cumberland Co. 1780/ Father, George COLQUHOUN.

COLQUHOUN, William 1796/ in 1820 census in Washington Co., PA. Sailed to US in May, 1818.

COLQUOHON, Charles Richmond Co., NC No twp listed 1795.

COLQUOHON, John Richmond Co., NC No twp listed 1795.

IMMIGRANTS FROM SCOTLAND AND IRELAND

CAHOON, William s/o Sir Alexander COLQUHOUN came from Scotland to Taunton, Mass. in 1635 m/ Deliverence Peck and moved to Block Island.

CALHOUN, Adam Sr. and spouse, Violet Davis, daughter of George Davis, had son Adam CALHOUN, Jr. who patented several hundred acres on SC Branch of Buffaloe River in 1749. He sold 200 A. to his father in 1754. They were members of Briery Church. Adam, Jr. married Jane Daniels in 1799 and was ruling elder in church in 1819.

CALHOUN, Alexander 1726/ in Petersham, Worchester, Ma. married Eliner McFarland and were parents to Samuel CALHOUN 1761/ who married Lucy Gibbs: Daughter possibly Elizabeth CALHOUN 9, 3, 1794 in New Salem, Franklin County Ma. These were all related to Vice-President John C. CALHOUN of SC and to US Representative William Barron CALHOUN, and were progenitors of Cahoons who eventually settled in RI and

Va and perhaps in other New England states.

CALHOUN, Irvin age 43 and spouse Nancy age 37 had following children: John C. 14, James W. 13, Burrel R. 12, George L. 10, Dan O. 9, Emily E. 7, Clarissa h. 4, Charlton H. 3, Washington 1, Female (NN) 3 months. This from 1870 census from Montgomery County, Georgia.

CALHOUN, James 1716/1760, second child of Patrick CALHOUN and Catherine Montgomery, married 1736 Nancy Ann (Susannah) Long in Donegal, Ireland. James, Jr. was born in VA and had a son, Robert.

CALHOUN, James Sr. 1735 VA/1795 in Guilford Co., NC m/ Janet Johnston /1804 in Guilford Co., NC.

CALHOUN, James Jr. 1763 VA/ 1830 in Guilford Co., NC m/1790 to Sarah (NN) 1764/.

CALHOUN, Patrick 1723/1796, born in Ireland. Died in Abbeville, District, SC. Came to SC - served in the Legislature and was by profession a surveyor. In 1775 he was a member of the provincial Congress. He married second time to Martha Caldwell 1750/1802. Their son, Patrick, Jr. 1784/1840 m/ Nancy Needham De Graffenreid 1787/1841 in 1806. Their son, Ludlow CALHOUN 1818/1863 m/ Margaret Teague 1816/1858. They had daughter Permelia Ella CALHOUN 1856-1906 and son, William CALHOUN, great grandson, Thomas Jefferson

COLQUHOUN/CALHOUN

CALHOUN, , great grandson, William McCaw
CALHOUN father of Margaret Meek CALHOUN
Hughes who was born in Tallahatchie Co.,
MS.

CALHOUN, William 4,10,1793 Guilford Co.,
NC/1866 in Forsyth Co., NC. m/8,5,1829

COHOON, Joseph 1755/ was in Orange Co. NY
in 1790. He or son served in Revolutionary
War from Orange Co. He had nine sons by
two wives (NN). Some of the sons went to
Barbados.

COLQUHOUN, Agnes, Scotland, d/o Patrick
and Margaret m/1777 Archibald NcNaughten.

COLQUHOUN, Alexander was surgeon from
Edinburgh, Scotland in 1749.

COLQUHOUN, Angus, immigrant from Scotland
with wife, son and 3 daughters to Canada
on the ship, George Canning in June 1821.
Received land grant in Lanark, Upper
Canada on July 1821.

COLQUHOUN, Angus, born in Scotland
emigrated to American during 1790, settled
in SC 1805. He was naturalized 5,11,1806
in Marlbourough, SC.

COLQUHOUN, Ann age 20 to Wilmington, NC
1775.

COLQUHOUN, Ann Jane age 14 to Petersburg,
VA 1819.

COLQUHOUN, Archibald age 22, to Wilmington, NC 1775

COLQUHOUN, Archibald w/ wife, son, two daughters to Canada from Scotland. Received land grant Ramsey, Upper Canada on 8/16/1822. He was a farmer and Jacobite, resident of Appin Argyll from 3/1847. Went from Tibburg to Jamaica or Barbados in 1847.

COLQUHOUN, Archibald 1768 Scotland/ Emigrated to America 1802. Farmer in Richmond Co., NC w/ wife and two children 1812.

COLQUHOUN, Archibald, /8,7,1786. s/o James, Provost of Dumbarton,

COLQUHOUN, Barbary age 2, to Petersburg, VA 1819

COLQUHOUN, Clara Cleemans (McKee) 1,11,1852/5,8,1912 w/o Samuel T. McKee

COLQUHOUN, Frs A. Jr. age 11, to Petersburg, VA 1819.

COLQUHOUN, Ann age 36, to Petersburg, Va. 1819.

COLQUHOUN, Duncan 1760/ Scotland, emigrated to America in 1790. He was a cooper in Richmond Co., NC w/wife and eight children in 1812.

COLQUHOUN, James C. w/wife two sons, four daughters to Upper Canada from Scotland on

10/1/1820 on the ship "Commerce". Settled Lanark on a land grant.

COLQUHOUN, James C. w/wife, son and two daughter came to Canada from Scotland on the "George Canning for land grant in Lanark in northern Canada on 7/25/1821.

COLQUHOUN, John to Boston, Mass in 1651

COLQUHOUN, John to Philadelphia, PA in 1860.

COLQUHOUN, Mary age 12, to Petersburg, VA 1819.

COLQUHOUN, Robert from Glasgow on Merchant Ship to St. Kitts during 1700's.

COLQUHOUN, Robert to Philadelphia, PA in 1876.

COLQUHOUN, Roderick age 16 to Petersburg, VA in 1819.

COLQUHOUN, Thomas age 45 and Thomas R. age 6, to Petersburg, VA

COLQUHOUN, Walter C. 1788/came from RHU, to Hudson Bay ca/1813 and probably to Red River.

MARRIAGES

CAHOON, William 1633/6,22,1675 was killed during the first days of King Phillip's War) m/ Deliverance Peck. He s/o Alexander COLQUHOUN, who was s/o Sir Alexander

COLQUHOUN/CALHOUN

COLQUHOUN 15th and 17th of Luss, who was
s/o Sir John COLQUHOUN 13th KT and 15th of
Luss, who was s/o Sir Humphrey COLQUHOUN
12th and 14th of Luss. William Cahoon was
a brickmaker in Swansea, MA.

CALHOUN, Adam Sr. (sometimes spelled
Colquhoun) m/ Violet Davis, d/o George
Davis. Adam, Jr. s.o Adam Sr. and Violet
m/Jane Daniels in 1799 and was ruling
elder in the Briery Church in 1819. Adam,
Jr. patented several hundred acres on SC
branch of Buffaloe river in 1749 and sold
200 acres to his father in 1754

CALHOUN, Andrew Jackson 10,15,1836/ 10,8,
1863 of wounds from battle of Chicagmauga,
GA.

CALHOUN, Elisha /9,15,1879 m/Sarah Lester
4,21,1820 in SC/ 12,24,1858.

CALHOUN, Elizabeth D. 1837 MO/1860 MO m/
Thomas Sylvester Parsons 1837 LA/.

CALHOUN, James m/ Mary Lessly, d/o Thomas
Lessly on 2, 8, 1792.

CALHOUN, John m/Lurana Wall in 1799 in
Abbeville District,SC. Lurana died at
Catawba, Harris Co., GA and is buried in
unmarked grave while traveling to the new
family home in Russell Co.,Al. John died
when 75 years of age in Russell Co., Al.
leaving descendents around Columbus, GA
and Phoenix City, Al. Their children:John
7, 5, 1800/; Robert 10,6, 1801/12/13/1858
in Montgomery, Al,: Elisha 2,2,1804/;

COLQUHOUN/CALHOUN

Euphemia 5,12,1807/in Jones County, Georgia; Patrick M. 11,26,1808; Ezekiel 7.28, 1811/8,5,1847; Samuel born Bibb Co., GA; Rhoda Green 7, 19, 1815/; Maria 5, 11, 1820/.

CALHOUN, John L /5,5,1849 in Crawford Co., Al m/ Hannah Louise CALHOUN. Their children all born in GA: Ezekiel m/Lucretia Bazemore; Monroe m/Martha Franklin; Mary m/ William Hartwell Sims; Eliza m/Zach Sims; Sarah m/John Franklin; Patrick 1838/ recorded in 1850 census of Russell Co., AL as 12 years of age and b/ in GA; Thomas 1839/; Laura. At the death of John L. they lived with two of his bachelor brothers, Robert and Patrick. The will of Robert to Patrick was contested by all heirs of his estate and John W. Shields was appointed guardian for Laura, Thomas, Monroe, Elisha and Ezekiel CALHOUN.

CALHOUN, John 1855 VA/ m/1877 to Nancy, Crow 1859 VA/

CALHOUN, Marcus S. 1782 VA/m/ Elizabeth (NN) of Va.

CALHOUN, Permilia 1830 TN/1850 m/ Silas, Webb 1828 TN/.

CALHOUN, Phoebe m. James Reid 1765/

CALHOUN, Margaret 1785 SC/ m/ Richard Wilson 11,30,1802 in Oglethorpe Co., GA

CALHOUN, Patrick m/Sarah CALHOUN McKinley. (Sarah had daughter, who m/William Holmes) Children: John 1774/ m/Elissa Norris or Alice Morris; James, Sr. 1776/ was Sheriff, m/Rhoda Green. Their children: James, Jr.; and John m/Laurana Wall. Their son was Robert.

CALHOUN, Peter m/Helen (Ellen) McAuslan Children: John, Peter, Mary, Jeanette, Archibald, Helen, Malcolm, James, Daniel, Margaret (ND)

CALHOUN, Peter, Peter m/Mary McAuslan- her mother was a Gibbons.

CALHOUN, Samuel 1761/ m/Lucy Gibbs. His father was Alexander CALHOUN 1726/ in Petersham, Worcester Co. MA m/Eliner MCFarland. These Calhouns related to Vice-President, John C. CALHOUN of SC and US Representative William Barron CALHOUN, Progenitors of Cahoons who eventually settled in RI and Va and Possibly elsewhere in New England. Samuel and Lucy had another daughter Elizabeth CALHOUN 9,3,1794/ in New Salem Franklin Co., MA.

CALHOUN, William m/1,30,1805 Catherine Jenner de Graffenreid 6,9,1786/2,3,1829, sister of Nancy Needham, wife of his brother, Patrick CALHOUN.

CALHOUN, William Boyd 3,10,1818 /1,2,1891 m/first Maria Lavinia Beasley. Their children: Martha; Nathan 7,30,1839; Eugenia; Emma E. 11,6,1842/; Harriet "Hattie" Loraine 8,7,1847; Jessie Beasley

COLQUHOUN/CALHOUN

7, 10, 1849/7,8,1861. William Boyd CALHOUN m/second Matilda McSweeny, native of Maryland 1817/1867. Their children: Joseph died as infant, Lee.

CALHOUN, William A. 1824 VA/ m/1852 to Sarah J. Crow 1830 COLQUHOUN, Adam 1601/ m/Miss Lindsey of Bonhill. He, s/o Alexander COLQUHOUN, moved to Ireland.

COLQUHOUN, Alexander 1601/5,25,1617 m/Margaret Helen Buchanan, d/o Sir George Buchanan on 8,15,1595. He, s/o Sir John COLQUHOUN. Alexander and M. Helen's lineage: Adam 1601/; Robert 1622/; William 1643/; Rev. Alexander 1662/ m/ Judith Hamilton; William 1686/; Patrick I m/Catherine Montgomery (Reported to be one of the first three brothers to immigrate to PA in 1733); Mary Catherine 1714/1730 and son James 1716/1760; Patrick III 1737/ m/first Alice Craighead and second Sarah McKinley.

COLQUHOUN, Allan Bannatyne 10,10,1879 in Scotland/1972 m/Alice Nelson 7, 3,1882/ 1,23,1940. Allan changed his name to CALHOUN. Lived in Burma, India, and Minneapolis, MN. s/o David COLQUHOUN and Ann Bannatyne. Allan and Alice's children: Allen Nelson CALHOUN 8,20,1913/ m/Jean Young; Jean CALHOUN 11,13,1917/ m/ Dr. Fred Hayes. Allan m/ second Mabel Craig 9,24,1885/ No children from this marriage.

COLQUHOUN, Andrew Sutherland s/o John COLQUHOUN and Mary Mearns.

COLQUHOUN Ann, d/o John COLQUHOUN and Mary
Mearns COLQUHOUN,m/John Charles Walker
12/17/1839 (Will Dated)/.

COLQUHOUN, Charles C. m/Mary Balfour.
Their children were Sallie COLQUHOUN
9,22,1872/5,9,1912; William L. 12,19,1875/
9,4, 1882; James Roach 8,4,1877/

COLQUHOUN, Clara Cleemans m/ Samuel T.
McKee 1,10,1884 ceremony performed by Rev.
W. L. C. Honnicut. She d/o James and Mary
Francis Sulivan COLQUHOUN.

COLQUHOUN, David Sr., 11,12,1852 Edinburgh
Scotland/ 10,29,1908 m/Ann Bannatyne
5,16,1850 Glasgow, Scotland. They left
Greenock, Scotland in 1880 or 1881. Their
children: David COLQUHOUN 1,15,1878
Scotland/ 3,6,1940 Scotland m/Anne
Anderson of Norway; Allan COLQUHOUN
CALHOUN 10,10,1879/1972 m/ Alice Nelson;
Ann Talbot COLQUHOUN 11,12,1881/ 3,11,1958
Canada m/ Harry Sanger; Jane Robertson
COLQUHOUN 12,28,1883 MN/9,5,1968 m/ Frank
Morse; Maud COLQUHOUN 9,20,1886 m/ Lloyd
Hatcher; William COLQUHOUN 4,9,1889/
7,29,1890; James COLQUHOUN 5,30,1891/
5,25,1986 m/ Minnie Velin; Samuel
COLQUHOUN (changed name to CALHOUN)
10,31,1893/5,21,1974 m/Lillian Iverson;
Robert COLQUHOUN (changed name to CALHOUN)
9,17,1897/ m/ Geneva Heckey.

COLQUHOUN, David Jr. 1,15,1878 Scotland/
3,6,1940 m/Anne Anderson 1885 Norway
/12,31,1952. He s/o David COLQUHOUN and

COLQUHOUN/CALHOUN

Ann Bannatyne. Their children: Donald; David; Alfred; Samuel; Ann m/Melvin Huseby; Alice m/ Noah Palmer; Luella m/ Tiehm.

COLQUHOUN, Sir Humphrey /1536 m/ Lady Catherine Graham d/o William, first Earl of Montrose. He s/o Sir John COLQUHOUN.

COLQUHOUN, Sir Humphrey 1478/1493 m/first Jean Erskine and second Marion Baillie. He s/o Sir John COLQUHOUN.

COLQUHOUN, Janet 7,31,1839/11,9,1870 (d/o James COLQUHOUN and Mary Francis Sulivan COLQUHOUN) m/ Charles C. Balfour on 8,22,1863 in Montgomery, AL. Their children: James COLQUHOUN 1865/1865; Charles Clifton 5,8,1867/ ; Janet 12,17,1869.

COLQUHOUN, James 10,21,1858/ at High Church, Paisley, Renfrew Scotland m/ Elizabeth Meiklejohn.

COLQUHOUN, James 12,6,1748/ m/Jean COLQUHOUN.

COLQUHOUN, James 5,27,1864 at Meigh, Armagh, Ireland m/Bridget Morgan.

COLQUHOUN, James m/ Laura Mayfred Burpee (of garden fame). She had two brothers James, William- all living in Dundee, Quebec.

COLQUHOUN/CALHOUN

COLQUHOUN, James m/Martha Gatewood, parents of James and Mary Francis Sulivan COLQUHOUN (ND).

COLQUHOUN, Sir John 8th 1408/1439 m/ Jean Erskine

COLQUHOUN, Sir John 13th 1538/1574 m/first, Christian Erskine, d/o Lord Robert and wife Elizabeth Campbell Erskine, and m/second, Agnes Boyd, d/o of Robert, 4th Lord Boyd. Sir John was s/o Sir Humphrey.

COLQUHOUN, Sir John 9th 1439/1478 m/first Miss Boyd d/o Lord Thomas Boyd and m/second Elizabeth Dunbar. He, s/o Malcolm COLQUHOUN.

COLQUHOUN, Sir John 11th 1493/1536 m/Elizabeth or Margaret Stewart (Stuart) d/o John, Earl of Lennox.

COLQUHOUN, John m/Mary Mearns 6,9,1846 in Aberdeen St. Nicholas, Scotland.

COLQUHOUN, John 10,13,1709/1729 m/Jean Taylor. John's parents were John COLQUHOUN m/1707 to Elizabeth d/o James Donaldson who had four sons, John (above), James 5,17,1711/ Archibald 2,11,1713/ and Robert 1,5,1716/1787 m/Helen Johnston. John and Jean's children: Ludowick 1726/ and Robert, the ancestor of ROBERT COLQUHOUN RANDEL. Robert and wife (NN) had twin sons, Robert and James. James m/ Martha Gatewood. James and Martha were the grandparents of ROBERT COLQUHOUN RANDEL'S

COLQUHOUN/CALHOUN

ROBERT COLQUHOUN RANDEL

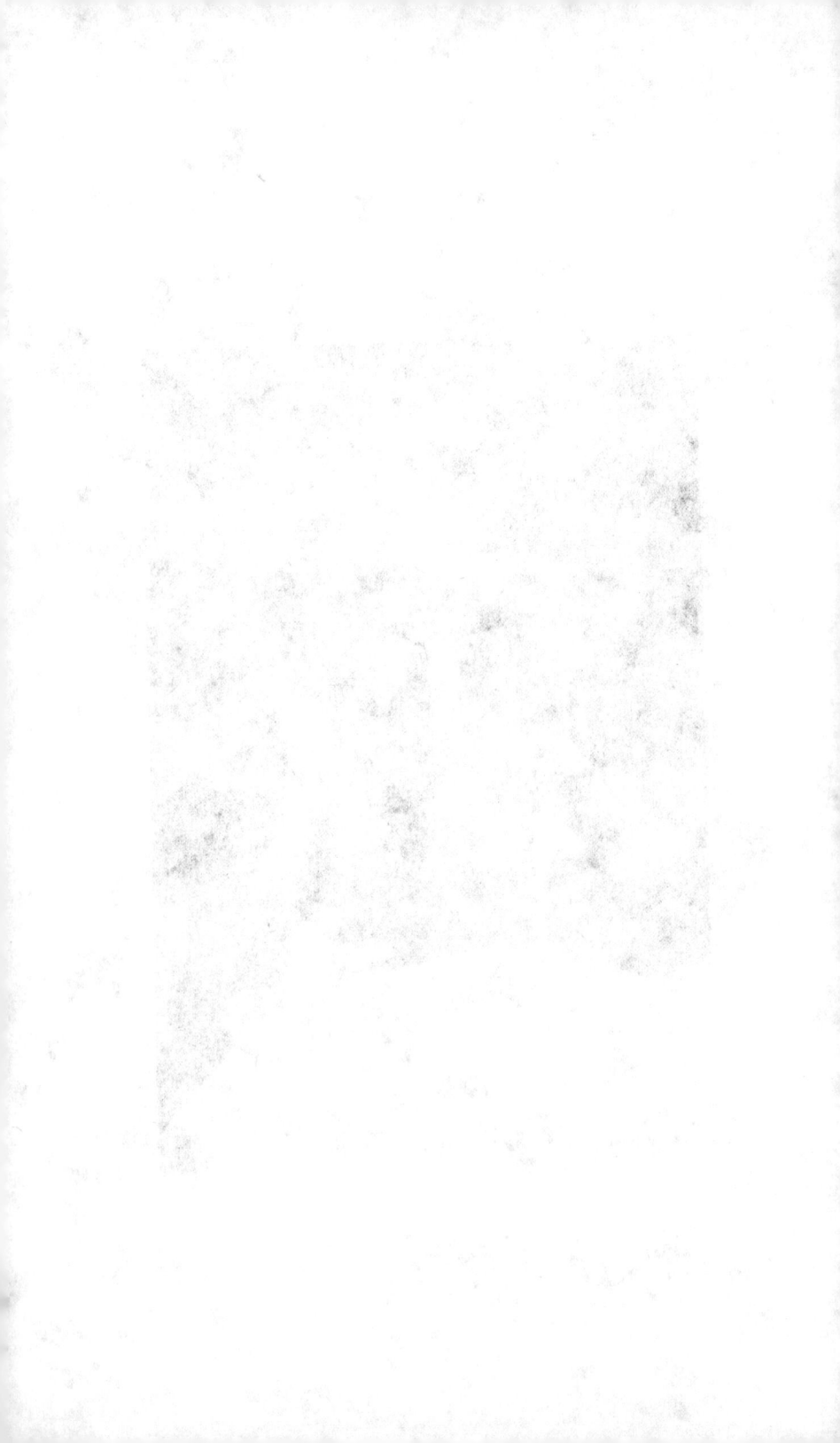

COLQUHOUN/CALHOUN

mother, MARTHA ANN COLQUHOUN. There were
many Gatewoods in NC and Va. There's a
small town of Gatewood in Caswell Co., NC
between Danville, VA and Yanceyville, NC.

COLQUHOUN, John 1763/12,28,1836 m/Helen
McLellan. He was son of Ludowick and
Christian. His children: Ludovic lived in
Texas, Left in Scotland were George and
Janet. There were others (NN).

COLQUHOUN, John 4,3,1790/ Glasgow, Lanark,
Scotland m/Euphan M'Kenzie.

COLQUHOUN, Ludowick 5,1726/ 7,28,1799
m/Christian McLellan. Their sons: John and
Walter.

COLQUHOUN, Malcolm /before 1459 spouse
(NN).

COLQUHOUN, Malcolm, Jr. came from Isle of
Skye, Scotland to VA in 1792 with father,
Malcolm and mother Christian McCorquodale.
She died in Grove Hill, Clarke Co., Al
March 3, 1828. These siblings all born on
Isle of Skye: Katherine (Kate) 1785/;
Nancy 1786/; John 6,27,1788/; These
siblings were born in VA: Duncan; Neal;
Mary; and Christian: This family moved to
Cumberland Co., NC and to Grove Hill,
Clarke Co., Al

COLQUHOUN, Malcolm Edward, s/o John
COLQUHOUN and Mary Mearns, m/ Eliza
Hazells 6/7/1874 in Aberdeen, Kintore,
Scotland.

195

COLQUHOUN, Margaret m/ James Morrison 5/1/1823 in Aberdeen, Scotland.

COLQUHOUN, Margaret m/ Hugh Crawford. She d/o Patrick COLQUHOUN of Tullichintaull and Isabel McCauley. They were living ca 1565. Hugh was born in Kilburne, Ayrshire, Scotland.

(Mother of ROBERT COLQUHOUN RANDEL) COLQUHOUN, Martha Ann 1,30,1841/6,22,1916 m/James Mason Randel on 7,12,1863 at Brandon, MS. She was daughter of James COLQUHOUN and Mary Francis Sulivan COLQUHOUN. Family history indicates James and Mary F. were born in Scotland, but no proof of same. They were married in Danville, VA on 12/24/1833, ceremony performed by Rev. Montgomery. Children: Mary Miranda Randel 10,25,1864/ 9,28,1866; James Randel 7,28,1866/ 4,21,1873; Walter Lee Randel 6,22,1868 William Wallace Randel 7,1,1871; Estelle Randel 9,29,1873; ROBERT COLQUHOUN RANDEL 7,9,1875/ 3,16,1963; Benjamin Randel 10,12,1880.

COLQUHOUN, Martha m/ General Nathaniel Greene after Revolutionary War. Greene Co., MS was organized out of Washington, Co., which spread from the Chatahootchee to the Mississippi River in 1811. (This was family report from ROBERT COLQUHOUN RANDEL).

COLQUHOUN, Mary d/o James and Mary Francis Sulivan COLQUHOUN m/ C. E. Balfour 10,3,1871, ceremony performed by Rev. M. Harris.

COLQUHOUN, Mary Morrison, d/o James
COLQUHOUN and Mary Mearns, m/ Robert
Traill 9,1,1875.

COLQUHOUN, Patrick,12,21,1714/ Dumbarton,
Scotland m/ Agnes McNair. He s/o Adam
COLQUHOUN.

COLQUHOUN, Patrick m/Catherine Montgomery
in 1683/4. They are considered the
progenitors of 85% of emigrants to the US.

COLQUHOUN, Patrick, 5,25,1690/ Old
Kilpatrick, Dumbarton, Scotland, m. Isobel
Graham: Their daughter, Agnes.

COLQUHOUN, Patrick, 9,3,1751/ Edinburgh
Parish, Scotland m/ Margaret Stewart.
Their daughter (NN) born in Midlothian,
Scotland.

COLQUHOUN, Patrick, (Lord Prov.) 1752/
Scotland m/ Janet COLQUHOUN.

COLQUHOUN, Peter 1842/ m/ Christina
Fergusson.

COLQUHOUN, Sir Robert 1300/1390 m/ Lady of
Luss, d/o and heir of Godfrey of Luss. She
probably the inspiration for Sir Walter
Scott's "Lady of the Lake".

COLQUHOUN, Robert 1622/ m/Katherine
MacCauseland, his first cousin. He s/o
Adam.

COLQUHOUN/CALHOUN

COLQUHOUN, Robert, s/o John COLQUHOUN and Mary Mearns, m/Euphemia Sutherland 5,2,1805.

COLQUHOUN, ROBERT 5,20,1729/ Cardross, Dumbarton, Scotland m/ Mary McNeil. Their daughter: Agnes.

COLQUHOUN, Robert 7,21,1808 Glasgow, and Lanark, Scotland m.Janet Mason.

COLQUHOUN, Robert m/Frances Mills, d/o Ann COLQUHOUN and William Cunningham Farley. Their daughter, Dorothy Farley came from Scotland in 1802 to Davidson Co., TN. She married Isaac Butler in Scotland. Lucy Ann Butler 1,10,1802/4,25,1872 d/o Dorothy and Isaac, m/John Macimillian Robinson 3,14,1800/ in Greenville, SC.

COLQUHOUN, Robert N. (twin) s/o James and Mary Francis COLQUHOUN 6,14, 1830/ 12,6,1890 m/Alice D. Latimer on 12,5,1865 w/ceremony performed by Rev. G. Andrews. Their children: Robert Latimer 1,20,1868/; Mary Ellen 12,18,1870/; James Daniel 7,31, 1873/8,16,1875; Fannie 8,1876/12,22,1877; Rufus Neely 1878/; Alice 1881/; Walter Winchester 1885/.

COLQUHOUN, Walter 1768/6,21,1813 m. Claramond Peter (Poter). He s/o Ludowick and Christian COLQUHOUN. Their children: Claramond 7,23,1802/4,26,1866 m Gustavous B. B. Cleemanns w/one son Thomas M. Cleemanns, and Ludovic m/Frances COLQUHOUN and lived in Texas.

COLQUHOUN/CALHOUN

COLQUHOUN, Walter 4,11,1840/ 8,23,1916. m/ Sally Unthank on 1,26,1881. Their children: Mary Bell 10,24,1882/; James 1,1885/4,3,1885; Walter Unthank 6,22, 1886/7,1,1949; Lizzie Neely 9,17,1888/ 7,28,1889; Robert Walker 1,2,1891/; James Norman 1,4,1897.

COLQUHOUN, William m/ Ann Rodney 5,11, 1865.

COLQUHOUN, William Robert 1841/ Scotland, m/Frances Horton.

TAX LIST AND COUNTY RECORDS- GEORGIA

COLQUHOUN, Angus on 1822 in COLQUHOUN District. He was also mentioned on 6,8,1824 and 6,8, 1825 and with commission for Justices of the Inferior Court 1813-1821.

COLQUHOUN, Edith age 12 was listed in 51st District G. M. in December, 1836.

COLQUHOUN, Hugh was on 1805-06 tax list. in 51st District. He had 3 slaves.

COLQUHOUN, James on 1822 list in Adams District.

COLQUHOUN, Thomas B age 16. and Mary Ann F. COLQUHOUN age 13 were listed in Capt. Ryals District or 275 R. M. October 1829 as children entitled to the benefits of the Poor School Fund.

COLQUHOUN, Thomas B. won lot 992-21-2 in 1832 Gold Land Lottery in Edwards District. He was on 1834 tax list in Ryals District.

COLQUHOUN, Winnifred was on 1828 tax list in Ryals District. She had 2 slaves, was guardian of her 3 children and 5 slaves. In 1822-23 tax roll in Ryals District she had one slave.

COLQUHOUN/CALHOUN

COLQUHOUN SONGS

The COLQUHOUN songs: "Caismeachd Chloinn a 'Chompaich" is a march tune the had as its English equivalent translation, "The COLQUHOUN'S MARCH".

"Ceann na Drochaide Bige was a gethering tune with English equivalent, "The Head of the Little Bridge".

COLQUHOUN heirs have through modern time been musically inclined.

COLQUHOUN/CALHOUN

SOURCES OF INFORMATION- SCOTLAND

Aberdeen and North East Scotland Family
History Society
647 King Street
Aberdeen AB2 1SB Scotland

Anglo-Scottish Family History Society,
Attention: Miss P. Connor
2 Beech St.;
Salford M6 4JF, England

Association of Scottish Genealogists and
Records Agents
P. O. Box 174
Edinburgh EH3 5QZ Scotland

Borders Family History Society
Attention: Mr. N. S. McLeish
Bumlea,
78 Weensland Rd.
Harwick TD9 9NX

Central Scotland Family History Society
29 Craiginnan Gardens,
Dollar FK14 7 JA

Dumfries & Galloway Family History Society
Attention: Mrs. Betty Watson
Kylelea, Corsook, Castle Douglas,
Kirkcudbrightshire DG7 3ON

Glasgow and West Scotland Family History
Society
Attention: Mr. J. K. Patrick
11 Cargows Crescent,
Falkirk FK1 5QH

COLQUHOUN/CALHOUN

Glasgow City Council
Libraries Department
The Mitchell Library
North Street
Glasgow G3 7DN Scotland
(This for births, baptisms, and marriages
prior to 1855)

Highland Family History Society
c/o The Reference Room
Public Library,
Farraline Park,
Inverness IV1 1NH

New Register House
Edinburgh EH1 3YY Scotland
(For births, deaths, and marriages after
1855)

SCOTLAND- General Register Office for
Scotland,
New Register House Edinburgh EH1 3YT,
Scotland

NEWSLETTER
Scottish History,
The Ellen Payne Odom Library
"The Family Tree"
P. O. Box 1110
Moultrie, GA 3177

Ordinance survey maps for Scotland
Free Irdubabce Survey,
Romsey Road, Maybush, Southhampton
Scotland SO9 4DH

Scots Ancestry Research Service
20 York Place

COLQUHOUN/CALHOUN

Edinburgh 1, Scotland

Scottish Genealogy Society,
21 Howard Pl.,
Edinburgh 3, Scotland

Scottish Tartans Society,
Museum of Scottish Tartans,
Comrie, Perthshire Scotland

Scots Ancestry Research Society
3 Albany Street
Edinburgh EH1 3PY Scotland

Tay Valley Family History Society, Hon.
Sec.,
c/o Carlton Gilruth Solicitors and
    Real Estate Agents
30 Whitehall St.
Dundee DD1 4A

The New York Caledonian Club, Inc.
P. O. Box 5967 Grand Central Station
NY, NY 10163-5967
Tel. 212-662-1083

Troon & District Family History Society,
c/o Miss Pat McCraig
37 South Beach,
Troon, Ayrshire KA10 6EF

COLQUHOUN/CALHOUN

SCOTTISH TERMS AND DEFINITIONS

BALMORAL- The flat "tam" type of headgear worn with the Highland Dress.

CABER- The 16-20 foot pole weighing between 80 and 100 pounds flipped end over end in the Caber Toss event.

CEILIDH- (Kay-Lee) A social gathering with singing, dancing and piping. A party.

CELTIC- An adjective referring to one of the early tribes of Scotland, such as Celtic art, Celtic language.

CHANTER- That part of the bagpipes, which the player holds with his hands to play the melody of the tune.

CLAN- A family unit, the Clan became the basic political, economic, and social unit of the Scottish Highlands until the political oppression of 1745.

DIRK- The short sword sometimes worn on the belt with Highland dress.

DRONE- One of the three "tubes" sticking out of a set of bagpipes. These provide the continuous tone unique to pipe music.

DRUM MAJOR- The marching leader of a pipe band. The drum major marches in front of the band and carries the mace.

GAELIC- The traditional language of the Scots.

GLENGARRY- The "fore and aft" type of headgear sometimes worn with Highland dress.

HIGHLANDS- That portion of Scotland which lies north of a line roughly between Glasgow and Edinburgh.

KILT- The traditional clothing of Scotland. Originally a large blanket wrapped around the body made from approximately six yards of material.

PIOBAIREACH- (Peeb Rock) The classical music of the great highland bagpipe consisting of a ground or basic theme with several variations.

PIPE MAJOR- The musical leader and usually the principal instructor.

PLAID- (Played) The blanket like garment worn over the shoulder by some in highland dress and was originally a part of the kilt.

SAINT ANDREW- The patron saint of Scotland. The first disciple of Christ, his bones were reported to rest in St. Andrew, Scotland.

SCOT- A noun referring to a person born in Scotland or of Scottish descent.

SCOTTISH- An adjective describing things pertaining to Scotland.

SEANN TRIUBHAS- (Sheen Truce) One of the traditional Highland Dances.

SEPT- A family not having the name of the clan, but associated with the clan and entitled to wear its tartan.

SGIAN DUBH- (Skeen Doo) The small knife worn in the hose top with Highland dress. Translated from Gaelic to mean "Black Knife" -its intended use and not its color.

SPORRAN- The pouch worn in the front of the kilt which serves as a purse or pocket.

SCOT BOOKS
For Genealogical Reference

"Ancestral Roots of Sixty Colonists"
(USA)

"Antiquarian Notes, Historical, Genealogical, and Social" by Fraser-Mackintosh, Charles, 1828-1901. Inverness-shire parish by parish. Inverness, A. & W MacKenzie, 1897.

"Burke's Landed Gentry"

"Charles Edward Stuart's Army, 1745-46" Editors, Alastair Livingstone, Christian W. H. Aikman, and Betty Stuart Hart; foreword by Sir Donald Cameron, K. R.; introduction by Bruce P. Lenman, Published Aberdeen, Scotland: Aberdeen University Press, 1984.

"The Clan Almanac" by Charles MacLean (concise but good to find the clans and septs of Clans)

"A Concise History of Scotland" by Fitzroy Maclean (tells of early history of Scotland and beginnings.

"On the Crofter's Trail- in Search of the Clearance Highlanders." by David Craig and published by Jonathan Cape, London 1990.

"Culloden and the '45 Black'" by Jeremy Published Gloucester, England: Alan

208

Sutton, 1990, xiv, 217 p.: ill.; Includes
bibliographical references /index.

"Debrett's Family Historian" a Guide to
Tracing Your Ancestry by Noel Currer-
briggs and Royston Gambier, Webb and Power
Limited 1981.

"A Genealogical Gazetteer of Scotland" by
Frank Smith.

"The Highland Clans" by Sir Iain
Moncreiffe of that Ilk and David Hicks.

"The Highland Clearances" by John Prebble.
Penguin books 1963.

"The History of the Highland Clearances by
Alexander MacKenzie (first published in
1883)

"History of the Highlands, and the
Highland Chiefs" Three volumes by James
Browne published in 1838. THIS ONE VERY
GOOD.

"A History of Scotland" by J. D. Mackie
Penguin Books (He was appointed H. M.
Historiographer in Scotland in 1958.
Scotland in 1958.

"Massacre of the Rosses" by Donald Ross

"Pocket Scots Dictionary" published by
Aberdeen Press

"The Ross and Cromarty Book" edited by
Donald Omand, published by the Northern

Times Limited.. Other similar references done on Caithness, Moray, and Sutherland.

"Royal Genealogies" by James Anderson.

"Scot Kith and Kin" Clan House of Edinburgh Ltd. (Clan names and associated families - publisher changes almost with each issue. ISBN # 0 00 435665 9).

"Scottish Clans & Tartans" by Ian Trimble (tells of Highland Clans- their beginning of Clan and history, shows pictures of Tartans.

"Scottish Lore and Folklore," compiled by Ronald MacDonald Douglas, Beekman House - (History, Cultural and other fun things Scottish).

"Scotland and Her Tartans" by Alexander Fulton (this contains history of some of earlier known Clans not so well known today).

"In Search of Scottish ancestry" by Gerald Hamilton-Edwards. 2nd impression (corr) London: Phillimore, 1973, c 1972.

"The Surnames of Scotland, their Origin, Meaning and History" by George F. Black, (Surnames, clans, tartans) NY Public Library, NY ISBN #0-87104-172-3.

"The Third Statistical Account of Scotland Vol. XIII. The County of Ross and Cromarty" They have also issued books on Inverness, Orkney, Shetland, Midlothian.

To be released are: Kincardine, Berwick, Caithness and Sutherland, Roxburgh, West Lothian. As they say in the Highlands they are a bit "pricey" at 37.5 pounds, but they are worth it. They devoted several pages of background and history and statistics about all of the Parishes within the County.

"Ulster emigration to Colonial America 1718-1775" R. J.

INDEX

CALDWELL, JAMES (CAPT.) 70
CALDWELL, MARTHA (1750) 184
CALGACUS (COLQUHOUN) 3, 4
CALHOUN, ADAM, SR. (CA 1750) 183, 188
CALHOUN, ADAM, JR. 183, 188
CALHOUN, AGNES 68
CALHOUN, ALEXANDER 68
CALHOUN, ALEXANDER (1726) 183, 190
CALHOUN, ALLAN COLQUHOUN (1879) 192
CALHOUN, ALLEN NELSON (1913) 191
CALHOUN, ANDREW JACKSON (1836) 188
CALHOUN, ANN 69
CALHOUN, ANNA MARIA 146
CALHOUN, ARCHIBALD 190
CALHOUN, BURREL R. (1858) 194
CALHOUN, CATHERINE 68
CALHOUN, CATHERINE D/O EZEKIEL 150
CALHOUN, CHARLTON H. (1867) 184
CALHOUN, CLARISSA (1866) 184
CALHOUN, DAN O. (1861) 184
CALHOUN, DANIEL 190
CALHOUN, DAVID 71, 175
CALHOUN, ELBERT CONLEY 175
CALHOUN, ELISHA (1804) 188, 189
CALHOUN, ELIZA 189
CALHOUN, ELIZABETH 70
CALHOUN, ELIZABETH (1794) 183, 190
CALHOUN, ELIZABETH D. (1837) 188
CALHOUN, EMILY E. (1863) 184
CALHOUN, EMMA E. (1842) 190
CALHOUN, ESTHER 68
CALHOUN, EUGENIA 190
CALHOUN, EUPHEMIA (1807) 189
CALHOUN, EZEKEIL (1733) 142, 150
CALHOUN, EZEKIAL 68, 69
CALHOUN, EZEKIEL 189
CALHOUN, EZEKIEL (1811) 189
CALHOUN, EZEKIEL S/O EXEKIEL 150

COLQUHOUN/CALHOUN

CALHOUN, FLORIDE 144
CALHOUN, GEORGE 148
CALHOUN, GEORGE L. (1860) 184
CALHOUN, HANNAH LOUISE 189
CALHOUN, HARRIET "HATTIE" LORAINE (1847)
     190
CALHOUN, HATTIE ANN (1873) 175
CALHOUN, HELEN 190
CALHOUN, IRVIN (1835) 184
CALHOUN, J. A. (1866) 175
CALHOUN, JAMES (CA1760) 168
CALHOUN, JAMES 190
CALHOUN, JAMES 68, 71,
CALHOUN, JAMES (1716) 184
CALHOUN, JAMES (1733) 142, 148, 149
CALHOUN, JAMES (CA1765) 188
CALHOUN, JAMES JR. (1763) 184, 190
CALHOUN, JAMES PATRICK (LATE 1600) 67
CALHOUN, JAMES SR. (1735) 184
CALHOUN, JAMES W. (1857) 184
CALHOUN, JAMES, SR. (1776) 190
CALHOUN, JANE 175
CALHOUN, JEAN (1917) 191
CALHOUN, JEAN W/O EZEKIEL 160
CALHOUN, JEANETTE 190
CALHOUN, JEANNE 149
CALHOUN, JESSIE BEASLEY (1849) 190
CALHOUN, JOHN 189
CALHOUN, JOHN 190
CALHOUN, JOHN 67
CALHOUN, JOHN 70
CALHOUN, JOHN (1733) 142
CALHOUN, JOHN (1774) 190
CALHOUN, JOHN (1800) 188
CALHOUN, JOHN (1855) 189
CALHOUN, JOHN (CA 1770) 188
CALHOUN, JOHN C. 67
CALHOUN, JOHN C. (1856) 184

215

CALHOUN, JOHN CALDWELL 141, 142, 143,
    144, 145, 146, 183, 190
CALHOUN, JOHN EWING 144, 150
CALHOUN, JOHN FRANKLIN 71
CALHOUN, JOHN KING 71
CALHOUN, JOHN L. (CA 1790-1800) 189
CALHOUN, JOSEPH 68, 191
CALHOUN, LAURA 189
CALHOUN, LEE 191
CALHOUN, LEVICIE (1860) 175
CALHOUN, LISSIE ANN (1879) 175, 176
CALHOUN, LUDLOW (1818) 184
CALHOUN, MALCOLM 190
CALHOUN, MARCUS S. (1782) 189
CALHOUN, MARGARET 190
CALHOUN, MARGARET (1785) 189
CALHOUN, MARGARET MEEK (HUGHES) 185
CALHOUN, MARIA (1820) 189
CALHOUN, MARTHA 191
CALHOUN, MARY 190
CALHOUN, MARY 68
CALHOUN, MARY (1733) 142, 143
CALHOUN, MARY BELLE 71
CALHOUN, MARY CATHERINE 67, 150
CALHOUN, MARY D/O EZEKIEL 150
CALHOUN, MARY M. (1868) 176
CALHOUN, MATTHEW 70
CALHOUN, MONROE 189
CALHOUN, MYREL 175
CALHOUN, NANCY (CA 1843) 183
CALHOUN, NATHAN (1839) 190
CALHOUN, PATRICK 190
CALHOUN, PATRICK 68
CALHOUN, PATRICK S/O EZEKIEL 150
CALHOUN, PATRICK (1723) 184
CALHOUN, PATRICK (1838) 189
CALHOUN, PATRICK (CA 1750) 189

CAMERON OF LOCHIEL   124
CAMERON, SIR DONALD   208
CAMPBELL, CHRISTIAN   OF GARSCUBE (1558)
    36, 162
CAMPBELL, COLIN 36, 39, 162, 163
CAMPBELL, ELIZABETH 36, 194
CAMPBELL, GENERAL JOHN OF BARBRECK   49,
    168
CAMPBELL, SIR DUNCAN 162
CAMPBELL, SIR DUNCAN OF AUCHINBRECK   41,
    164
CARLIPPIS, THOMAS 95
CARNAHAM, BETSEY 71
CARNEGIE, LORD DAVID 43
CARNEGIE, MAGDALEN 43
CATHCART, LORD ALLAN 5TH BARON 41, 164
CHAMBERLAINS, GREAT 26
CHIRNSIDE, WILLIAM 35, 162
CLEEMAN, THOMAS M. 153, 155, 198
CLEEMANN, LUDOVIC C. ATTORNEY 152, 153,
    154, 155, 156
CLEEMANNS, GUSTAVOUS B. B.   198
CLEEMANN, LUDOVIC 198
CLEGHORN-DAVIS, MARY 165
CLEMSON, COLONEL THOMAS GREEN 146
CLERK, SIR JAMES 102
COHOON, ANGUS 164
COHOON, ARCHIBALD 164
COHOON, CAPTAIN JOHN (1673) 165
COHOON, DELAWARE 165
COHOON, JAMES (1671) 165
COHOON, JAMES (1864) 173
COHOON, JOSEPH (1665) 165
COHOON, JOSEPH (1755) 185
COHOON, MARY (1664) 165
COHOON, NATHANIEL (1675) 165
COHOON, SAMUEL (1663) 165
COHOON, WILLIAM (1633) 165

COLQUHOUN, ALEXANDER   191
COLQUHOUN, ALEXANDER   (CA 1775)   179
COLQUHOUN, ALEXANDER, SURGEON 169, 185
COLQUHOUN, ALEXANDER   174
COLQUHOUN, ALEXANDER   179
COLQUHOUN, ALEXANDER   184
COLQUHOUN, ALEXANDER   187
COLQUHOUN, ALEXANDER (1573)   37
COLQUHOUN, ALEXANDER   190
COLQUHOUN, ALEXANDER (1601) 164, 191
COLQUHOUN, ALEXANDER (1669) 60
COLQUHOUN, ALEXANDER (1709)   46
COLQUHOUN, ALFRED   193
COLQUHOUN, ALICE   193
COLQUHOUN, ALICE (1881)   65, 198
COLQUHOUN, ALICE MURTHWAITE   174
COLQUHOUN, ALLAN BANNATYNE CALHOUN (1870)
    192
COLQUHOUN, ANDREW (1654)   67
COLQUHOUN, ANDREW SUTHERLAND (1847)   173
COLQUHOUN, ANDREW   SUTHERLAND   S/O   MARY
    MEARNS   191
COLQUHOUN, ANGUS   185
COLQUHOUN, ANGUS   171
COLQUHOUN, ANGUS (CA 1800)   185
COLQUHOUN, ANGUS (CA 1800)   199
COLQUHOUN, ANN (1755)   185
COLQUHOUN, ANN (1783)   186
COLQUHOUN, ANN (CA 1819)   173, 186
COLQUHOUN, ANN C/O MARY MEARNS   191
COLQUHOUN, ANN D/O DAVID, JR.   193
COLQUHOUN, ANN JANE (1805)   185
COLQUHOUN, ANN TALBOT   (1881) 176, 192
COLQUHOUN, ANNA (1588)   163
COLQUHOUN, ANNA (CA1590) 39
COLQUHOUN, ANNE   (CA 1735)   47
COLQUHOUN, ANNE (1746)   49, 168

COLQUHOUN, ANNE (GRANT) 45, 46, 47, 74,
    95, 119, 167
COLQUHOUN, ANNE. (CA1736) 46
COLQUHOUN, ARCHEBALD 182
COLQUHOUN, ARCHIBALD (CA 1500) 35
COLQUHOUN, ARCHIBALD (CA 1500) 33
COLQUHOUN, ARCHIBALD (CA 1800) 172
COLQUHOUN, ARCHIBALD 68
COLQUHOUN, ARCHIBALD (1713) 194
COLQUHOUN, ARCHIBALD (1715) 167
COLQUHOUN, ARCHIBALD (1753) 186
COLQUHOUN, ARCHIBALD (1768) 186
COLQUHOUN, ARCHIBALD (CA 1795) 185
COLQUHOUN, ARCHIBALD S/O JAMES 185
COLQUHOUN, ARTHUR HUGH (1875) 176
COLQUHOUN, BARBARY (1817) 186
COLQUHOUN, BEBECCA 182
COLQUHOUN, BURGESS ARCHIBALD 171
COLQUHOUN CARL DAVID (1916) 176, 178
COLQUHOUN, CAPTAIN R. N. (CA1725) 47
COLQUHOUN, CATHERINE W/O DRUMMOND 165
COLQUHOUN, CATHERINE (CA 1760) 49
COLQUHOUN, CATHERINE 43
COLQUHOUN, CATHERINE W/O MURE (1607) 164
COLQUHOUN, CATHERINE (1749) 168
COLQUHOUN, CATHERINE OF ARROCHAR (1516)
    35, 162
COLQUHOUN, CHARLES ALEXANDER 156
COLQUHOUN, CHARLES CATHART (1723) 47
COLQUHOUN, CHARLES CLIFTON (1867) 65,
    66, 193
COLQUHOUN, CHARLES GORDON (1859) 176
COLQUHOUN, CHIEF JOHN 6TH OF CAMSTRADDEN
    29,
COLQUHOUN, CHRISTIAN 195
COLQUHOUN, CHRISTIAN D/O ROBERT 60
COLQUHOUN, CHRISTIAN (CA 1800) 194
COLQUHOUN, CHRISTIAN M/ALEXANDER 59

COLQUHOUN/CALHOUN

COLQUHOUN, CHRISTIAN MCLELLAN 155
COLQUHOUN, CHRISTIAN NOBLE (1871) 176
COLQUHOUN, CHRISTIAN OF GLENGARNOCK
   (1375) 30, 161
COLQUHOUN, CHRISTIBELL 62, 176
COLQUHOUN, CLARA CLEEMANS (1852) 62,
   65, 186, 192
COLQUHOUN, CLARAMOND (1802) 198
COLQUHOUN, CLEMENTINE (CA 1730) 47
COLQUHOUN, CORPORAL SUTHERLAND MORRISON
   51
COLQUHOUN, DAVID (1878) 191
COLQUHOUN, DAVID 174
COLQUHOUN, DAVID 178
COLQUHOUN, DAVID 191
COLQUHOUN, DAVID 192
COLQUHOUN, DAVID (1852) 180
COLQUHOUN, DAVID JR, (1878) 192
COLQUHOUN, DAVID, SR. (1852) 192
COLQUHOUN, DONALD 193
COLQUHOUN, DUNCAN (1760) 186
COLQUHOUN, DUNCAN 195
COLQUHOUN, EDITH (1824) 199
COLQUHOUN, ELIZABETH (CA 1500) 35
COLQUHOUN, ELIZABETH (CA 1727) 47
COLQUHOUN, ELIZABETH OF POLMAISE (CA1500)
   33
COLQUHOUN, ELIZABETH OF KEPPS 45
COLQUHOUN, EMILIE 178
COLQUHOUN, EMELINE (1843) 62
COLQUHOUN, ERNEST CECIL (1874) 177
COLQUHOUN, ESTELLE (1850) 62, 177
COLQUHOUN, EZEKIEL S/O PATRICK AND
   CATHERINE 166
COLQUHOUN, FANNIE (1876) 65, 198
COLQUHOUN, FRANCES 198
COLQUHOUN, FRANCIS 1717) 47
COLQUHOUN, FREDERICK (CA 1775) 181

222

COLQUHOUN, JAMES (1714) 47
COLQUHOUN, JAMES (1716)   S/O PATRICK &
CATHERINE 167, 191
COLQUHOUN, JAMES (1748)   193
COLQUHOUN, JAMES (1758)   169
COLQUHOUN, JAMES (1765) 169, 177
COLQUHOUN, JAMES (1774) ROSENEATH 169,
    177
COLQUHOUN, JAMES (1788)   177
COLQUHOUN, JAMES (1797)   171, 177
COLQUHOUN, JAMES H/O GATEWOOD 61, 194
COLQUHOUN, JAMES (1809)   61, 64, 150,
      151, 152, 153, 154, 176, 177,
      178, 179, 180, 181, 182, 192,
      193, 195, 196, 198
COLQUHOUN, JAMES (1858)   173, 193
COLQUHOUN, JAMES (1865)   193
COLQUHOUN, JAMES (1865)   65
COLQUHOUN, JAMES (1885)   66, 199
COLQUHOUN, JAMES (1891)   178, 192
COLQUHOUN, JAMES (CA 1500) 34
COLQUHOUN, JAMES (CA 1755) 179, 193
COLQUHOUN, JAMES (CA 1775)   176
COLQUHOUN, JAMES (CA 1780)   180, 181
COLQUHOUN, JAMES (CA 1780)   199
COLQUHOUN, JAMES (CA1570)   58
COLQUHOUN, JAMES (CA1765)   170
COLQUHOUN, JAMES ALEXANDER OF TULLYCHEWEN
    42
COLQUHOUN, JAMES C. (CA 1800)   172, 186,
    187
COLQUHOUN, JAMES D. (1830)   61, 62, 150,
    177
COLQUHOUN, JAMES DANIEL (1873)   65, 198
COLQUHOUN, JAMES NORMAN (1897)   66, 199
COLQUHOUN, JAMES OF BELVIE   43
COLQUHOUN, JAMES OF GARSCUBE (1517) 36,
    162

COLQUHOUN/CALHOUN

COLQUHOUN, JAMES PATRICK (1686) 166
COLQUHOUN, JAMES ROACH (1877) 66, 192
COLQUHOUN, JAMES S/O PATRICK & CATHERINE
    166
COLQUHOUN, JAMES, JR. GR S/O PATRICK &
    CATHERINE 166
COLQUHOUN, JANE (CA 1789) 51
COLQUHOUN, JANE (1751) 169
COLQUHOUN, JANE (1788) 171
COLQUHOUN, JANE OF FIFE (CA 1770) 49
COLQUHOUN, JANE ROBERTSON (1883) 192
COLQUHOUN, JANET (1746/7) 168
COLQUHOUN, JANET (CA 1800) 195
COLQUHOUN, JANET (1839) 62, 65, 193
COLQUHOUN, JANET (1869) 65, 193
COLQUHOUN, JANET (CA 1724) 47
COLQUHOUN, JANET (CA 1749) 49
COLQUHOUN, JEAN OF AUCHINBRECK 41
COLQUHOUN, JEAN OF BANNACHRA (CA 1592)
    39
COLQUHOUN, JEAN OF TULLICHEWAN (CA
    1580) 42
COLQUHOUN, JEAN (CA 1732) 47
COLQUHOUN, JEAN OF MINTO (1569) 37, 162
COLQUHOUN, JEAN 169
COLQUHOUN, JEAN 193
COLQUHOUN, JEAN OF ABERCORN (1605) 164
COLQUHOUN, JEAN (1630) 165
COLQUHOUN, JEAN (CA 1625) 39, 42
COLQUHOUN, JEAN EWING 176
COLQUHOUN, JOHN (1780) 169
COLQUHOUN, JOHN (1788) 195
COLQUHOUN, JOHN (1827) 178
COLQUHOUN, JOHN (1864) 177
COLQUHOUN, JOHN (1870) 178
COLQUHOUN, JOHN 179
COLQUHOUN, JOHN 182
COLQUHOUN, JOHN 194

225

COLQUHOUN, LADY HELEN SUTHERLAND 104,
   168
COLQUHOUN, LILLAS (1631) 43, 165
COLQUHOUN, LIZZIE NEELY (1888) 66, 199
COLQUHOUN, LUCY LEE (1848) 62, 178
COLQUHOUN, LUDOVICK (1757) 49, 169
COLQUHOUN, LUDOVICK S/O JOHN & JEAN 61
COLQUHOUN, LUDOVICK (CA 1784) 51
COLQUHOUN, LUDOWICK & CHRISTIAN 195,
   198
COLQUHOUN, LUDOWICK (1726) 195
COLQUHOUN, LUDVIC (1856) 62
COLQUHOUN, LUDVIC 178
COLQUHOUN, LUELLA 193
COLQUHOUN, M. C. 177, 181
COLQUHOUN, MALCOLM (1395) 31, 161
COLQUHOUN, MALCOLM (CA 1400) 195
COLQUHOUN, MALCOLM 194
COLQUHOUN, MALCOLM 72, 160
COLQUHOUN, MALCOLM (1764) 169
COLQUHOUN, MALCOLM EDWARD 195
COLQUHOUN, MALCOLM, JR 195
COLQUHOUN, MARGARET (1748) 168
COLQUHOUN, MARGARET (CA 1800) 195
COLQUHOUN, MARGARET OF DUNTREATH (1574)
   37, 39, 163
COLQUHOUN, MARGARET (CA1725) 47
COLQUHOUN, MARGARET (CA1770) 171
COLQUHOUN, MARGARET 177
COLQUHOUN, MARGARET D/O ROBERT 5TH LAIRD
   CAMSTRADDEN 59
COLQUHOUN, MARGARET TULLIBARDINE 32
COLQUHOUN, MARGARET (CA1750) 49
COLQUHOUN, MARGARET D/O ROBERT 5TH LAIRD
   58
COLQUHOUN, MARGARET W/O HUGH CRAWFORD 172, 196
COLQUHOUN, MARION OF GLASGOW (1513)
   34, 161

COLQUHOUN, NEAL 195
COLQUHOUN, PATRICK (CA 1590) 59
COLQUHOUN, PATRICK 167
COLQUHOUN, PATRICK 174
COLQUHOUN, PATRICK, LORD PROVOST 197
COLQUHOUN, PATRICK B/O SIR HUMPHREY 6TH
29
COLQUHOUN, PATRICK & MARGARET 170, 185
COLQUHOUN, PATRICK (1519) 162
COLQUHOUN, PATRICK (1604) 179
COLQUHOUN, PATRICK (1690) 167, 197
COLQUHOUN, PATRICK (1714) 197
COLQUHOUN, PATRICK (1751) 169, 197
COLQUHOUN, PATRICK (CA 1470) 33
COLQUHOUN, PATRICK (CA 1550) 36
COLQUHOUN, PATRICK (CA 1782) 50
COLQUHOUN, PATRICK (CA1350) 57
COLQUHOUN, PATRICK I (SR.) 166, 167, 191,
197
COLQUHOUN, PATRICK III (1737) 168, 191
COLQUHOUN, PATRICK JR. S/O PATRICK &
CATHERINE 166, 167
COLQUHOUN, PATRICK OF GLENNIS 30
COLQUHOUN, PATRICK OF TULLICHINTAULL 196
COLQUHOUN, PATRICK, LORD PROV. (1752)
197
COLQUHOUN, PETER (1842) 197
COLQUHOUN, PETER LUDOVIC (1776) 179
COLQUHOUN, REBECCA 182
COLQUHOUN, REGINALD 178
COLQUHOUN, REV. ALEXANDER (1622) 166,
180, 191
COLQUHOUN, REV. JOHN (1511) 34, 161
COLQUHOUN, ROBERT LATIMER (1868) 65,
198
COLQUHOUN, ROBERT (1452) 179
COLQUHOUN, ROBERT (1716) 194
COLQUHOUN, ROBERT 61

COLQUHOUN, ROBERT (CA 1725) 194
COLQUHOUN, ROBERT (1332) 179
COLQUHOUN, ROBERT (1356) 179
COLQUHOUN, ROBERT (1563) 59
COLQUHOUN, ROBERT (1622) S/O ADAM 166,
     191, 197
COLQUHOUN, ROBERT (1642) 60
COLQUHOUN, ROBERT (1729) 198
COLQUHOUN, ROBERT (1808) 172, 198
COLQUHOUN, ROBERT (CA 1610) 41
COLQUHOUN, ROBERT (CA 1700'S?) 187
COLQUHOUN, ROBERT (CA 1740) 176, 177
COLQUHOUN, ROBERT (CA 1850) 187
COLQUHOUN, ROBERT (CALHOUN) (1897) 192
COLQUHOUN, ROBERT (1622) 166, 190
COLQUHOUN, ROBERT 1ST LAIRD CAMSTRADDEN
     29, 57, 58, 160
COLQUHOUN, ROBERT 3RD LAIRD CAMSTRADDEN
     (1441) 58
COLQUHOUN, ROBERT 5TH LAIRD CAMSTRADDEN
     (1503) 59
COLQUHOUN, ROBERT 6TH LAIRD CAMSTRADDEN
     (1525) 59
COLQUHOUN, ROBERT BISHOP OF ARGYLL 32
COLQUHOUN, ROBERT C. 171
COLQUHOUN, ROBERT HAZLITT 157
COLQUHOUN, ROBERT LATIMER (1868) 64,
     198
COLQUHOUN, ROBERT N. (TWIN) 61, 62, 65,
     151, 152, 153, 154, 155, 177,
     176, 180, 181, 198
COLQUHOUN, ROBERT OF CAMSTRADDEN (1346)
     158
COLQUHOUN, ROBERT S/O ADAM (1808) 171
COLQUHOUN, ROBERT S/O MARY MEARNS 198
COLQUHOUN, ROBERT VII 29
COLQUHOUN, ROBERT WALKER (1891) 66, 199
COLQUHOUN, ROBERT, (1356) 178

232

COLQUHOUN, WILLIAM (1643) 164, 166,
    168, 180, 184, 191
COLQUHOUN, WILLIAM (1742) 168
COLQUHOUN, WILLIAM (1806) 53, 172, 178
COLQUHOUN, WILLIAM (1889) 191, 192
COLQUHOUN, WILLIAM 141
COLQUHOUN, WILLIAM 172
COLQUHOUN, WILLIAM (1796) 183
COLQUHOUN, WILLIAM (CA 1741) 49
COLQUHOUN, WILLIAM (CA 1780) 50
COLQUHOUN, WILLIAM (CA 1840) 199
COLQUHOUN, WILLIAM (CALHOUN) (1796) 171
COLQUHOUN, WILLIAM (SCOT) 154, 155
COLQUHOUN, WILLIAM H. SHELTON (1837) 62,
    181
COLQUHOUN, WILLIAM HANSON (1807) 181
COLQUHOUN, WILLIAM L. (1875) 66, 192
COLQUHOUN, WILLIAM OF GARSCADDEN 49, 169
COLQUHOUN, WILLIAM ROBERT (1841) 181,
    199
COLQUHOUN, WILLIAM S/O PATRICK &
    CATHERINE 166, 169, 180, 190
COLQUHOUN, WINNIFRED (CA 1790) 200
COLQUHOUN, ZULA MAE (1909) 181
COLQUHOUNE, ROBERT DE 25
COLQUOHON, CHARLES 182, 183
COLQUOHON, JOHN 182, 183
COLQUOUN, ANN EVANS (1844) 181
COMYN, SIR JOHN 19
CONACH 4
CONNOR, MISS P. 202
COUNTESS OF MARR 88
CONOCK 4
CRAIG, DAVID 208
CRAIG, MABEL (1885) 191
CRAIGHEAD, ALICE 168, 191
CRAWFORD, HUGH 67, 174, 196
CRAWFORD, JEAN (CA 1650) 67

CROCKETT, DAVY 141
CROMWELL, OLIVER 32, 93, 138
CROW, NANCY (1859) 189
CROW, SARAH J. (1830) 191
CULCHON, ROBERT DE 25
CUNNINGHAM, ALEXANDER EARL 161, 162
CUNNINGHAM, ALEXANDER, EARL OF GLENCAIRN
    38
CUNNINGHAM, DOROTHY FARLEY (1802) 171
CUNNINGHAM, ELIZABETH 59
CUNNINGHAM, JAMES 33, 36, 44, 161, 162
CUNNINGHAM, LADY CATHERINE 44
CUNNINGHAM, LADY JEAN (CA 1570) 38, 162
CUNNINGHAM, MARGARET 161
CUNNINGHAM, MARGARET OF CRAIGENDS 33, 54
CUNNINGHAM, PENUEL 44, 165
CUNNINGHAM, SIR JAMES OF GLENGARNOCK, 44
CUNNINGHAN, WILLIAM OF BALLYACHEN IRELAND
    44, 160, 165,
CUNNINGHAM, WILLIAM OF CRAIGENDS 35
CURRER-BRIGGS, NOEL 209
DANIELS, JANE 183, 187
DARNLEY, HENRY, LORD OF LENNOX 86, 87,
    88
DAVID, MARGARET D/O LORD 163
DAVIS, GEORGE 188
DAVIS, VIOLET 183, 188
DAY, LARRY HALE 64
DAY, LAURA ELLEN (1969) 64
DAY, LEE ANGELA (PINNIX) (1962) 64
DAY, SANDRA LYNN (1961) 64
DENZELESTOUN, ELIZABETH 60
DENZELESTOUN, ROBERT 60
DHU, JOHN 60
DONALDSON, JAMES D/O JAMES D. 194
DOUGLAS, DAVID 31
DOUGLAS, MARY 54
DOUGLAS, RONALD MACDONALD 210

LUSS, SIR JOHN 27
LUSS, THE LADY OF 72, 73
M'KENZIE, EUPHAN (CA 1795) 170, 195
MAC A CHOMBAICH (GAELIC) 4
MAC A CHOUNICH (GAELIC) 4
MACACHENNICK (GAELIC) 4
MACALPIN, DUNCAN 9
MACALPIN, KENNETH 8
MACALPIN, MARGARET 9
MACAULAY OF ARDENCAPLE 39, 98
MACCAUSELAND, CATHERINE (1643) 164, 180,
    197
MACCAUSLAND, KATHERINE 164
MACFARLANE, CHRISTIAN 58
MACFARLANE, DUNCAN OF ARROCHAR (1516)
    35, 162
MACFARLANE, WALTER 58
MACGREGOR, ALASTAIR 79, 83, 84
MACGREGOR, DUNCAN 78
MACGREGOR, IAIN DUBH (JOHN) 79, 83
MACGREGOR, IAINGLAS, CHIEF 80
MACGREGOR, ROB ROY 81, 82, 98, 119, 120,
    122, 123
MACINTIRE, BARBARA CAMILLA 49, 169
MACINTIRE, REV. DR. 49, 169
MACKENZIE, ALEXANDER 209
MACKENZIE, SIR, BARONET OF SCATWELL 49,
    1687
MACKIE, J. D. 209
MACLEAN, CHARLES 208
MACLEAN, FITZROY 208
MACNAUGHTON, DUNCAN MORE 58
MACPHERSON 15
MACROGER, JOHN 58
MAITLAND, FRANCES SARAH 52, 54, 74, 173
MAITLAND, SARAH (1802) 53, 173
MALCOLM I 8
MALCOLM II 8

241

MALCOLM III 9
MALCOLM, FOURTH EARL OF LENNOX 26
MALCOMN, FIFTH EARL OF LENNOX 26
MALDOUEN, THIRD EARL OF LENNOX 24
MALDOWEN, EARL OF LEVENAX 25
MANAY, CHARLES 40
MARJORIE, COUNTESS OF CARRICK 18
MARY MIRANDA RANDEL (1864) 196
MARY OF GUISE 86
MARY, QUEEN OF SCOTS 12, 35, 36, 37, 38,
    80, 86, 81, 86, 87, 88, 89, 97, 103
MASON, JANET 172, 176
MATTHEWS, AGNES 69
MATTHEWS, ALEXANDER 69
MATTHEWS, CAROLINE 69
MATTHEWS, ELIZABETH 69
MATTHEWS, ESTHER 69
MATTHEWS, EZEKIAL 68, 69
MATTHEWS, JANE 69
MATTHEWS, JOHN 69
MATTHEWS, JOSEPH 69, 70
MATTHEWS, JOSEPH CALHOUN 69
MATTHEWS, LAUREN 70
MATTHEWS, LUCRETIA 70
MATTHEWS, MARGARET 70
MATTHEWS, MARY 69
MATTHEWS, NANCY 69
MATTHEWS, PATRICK 69
MATTHEWS, RACHEL 69
MATTHEWS, THOMAS 69
MATTHEWS, WILLIAM 69
MAXWELL, JEAN 58
MCALISTER, ALEXANDER 141
MCALISTER, ELIZABETH 169
MCAUSELAN, JOHN 41, 162
MCAUSLAN, HELEN (ELLEN) 189
MCAUSLAN, MARY D/O GIBBONS 189
MCCAULEY, ALEX 60

COLQUHOUN/CALHOUN

MCCAULEY, ISABEL 174, 196
MCCAULEY, MARY 60
MCCLELLAND, MARTHA 71
MCCORQUODALE, CHRISTIAN 169, 195
MCCRAIG, MISS PAT 204
MCFARLAND, ELINER 183, 190
MCILHANEY, REV. JAMES 145
MCKEE, SAMUEL T. 65, 186, 192
MCKINLEY, SARAH 168, 191
MCKINLEY, SARAH CALHOUN 190
MCLEISH, MR. N. S. 202
MCLELLAN, CHRISTIAN (CA 1730) 195
MCLELLAN, HELEN 194
MCNAIR, AGNES 167
MCNAUGHTEN, ARCHIBALD (CA 1750) 185
MCNEIL, MARY 167
MCNEIT, MARY 197
MCSWEENY, MATILDA 191
MEARNS, MARY (1846) 173, 178, 191, 192,
    194, 195, 197
MEIKLEJOHN, ELIZABETH 172, 193
MERCHANT, KATHERINE 63
MILLS, FRANCES 197
MONCREIFFE, SIR IAIN 209
MONROE, PRESIDENT 144
MONTGOMERY, CATHERINE (CALHOUN) (1683)
    68, 142, 148, 149, 150, 165, 166,
    184, 191, 196
MONTROSE, MARQUIS 42, 73, 95
MONTROSE, JANET 60
MONTROSE, JOHN 4TH EARL 42
MONTROSE, MARQUIS OF 93, 94
MONTROSE, WILLIAM GRAHAM, EARL OF 72,
    160
MORGAN, BRIDGET 173, 193
MORRIS, ALICE 190
MORRISON, JAMES 196
MORSE, FRANK 192

COLQUHOUN/CALHOUN

COLQUHOUN/CALHOUN

RANDEL, ESTELLE (1873) 63, 196
RANDEL, JAMES (1866) 63, 196
RANDEL, JAMES MASON 62, 153, 154, 196
RANDEL, MARTHA ANN (BLUM) 63
RANDEL, MARY MIRANDA (1864) 63, 196
RANDEL, ROBERT COLQUHOUN 28, 57, 60, 61,
    62, 63, 72, 152, 157, 160, 194,   195,
    196,
RANDEL, THOMAS 63
RANDEL, WALTER LEE (1866) 63, 196
RANDEL, WILLIAM WALLACE (1871) 62, 196
READE, JOHN PAGE OF SUTTON HOUSE 53, 172
READE, JOHN, S/O JOHN PAGE 53
REEVE, TAPPING 143
REID, JAMES (1765) 189
RICH, MARY 165
RIZZIO, DAVID 87
ROBINSON, JOHN MACIMILLIAM 197
RODNEY, ANN 173, 199
ROSS, DONALD 209
SAINT KESSOG 97, 98
SANGER, HARRY CHEADLE 176, 192
SCHNEIDER, SANDRA LEE HUNING 64
SCHUBERT 109
SCOTA, D/O PHAROAH 2
SCOTT, SIR WALTER 26, 27, 52, 77, 81,
    82, 84, 109, 110, 111, 121, 122,
    123, 197
SEMPILE, ELIZABETH 58
SEMPILE, ROBERT 58
SHAKESPEARE 110
SHIELDS, JOHN W. 188, 189
SIMS, WILLIAM HARTWELL 189
SIMS, ZACH 189
SINCLAIR, JANET OF ULBSTER (1781) 51, 75,
    170
SINCLAIR, SIR JOHN 51, 170
SMITH, FRANK 209

245